CW01080551

WITHOUT WINGS

THE STORY OF HITLER'S AIRCRAFT CARRIER

BY

STEPHEN BURKE

Order this book online at www.trafford.com/07-0617
or email orders@trafford.com

Most Trafford titles are also available at major online book retailers.

© Copyright 2007 Stephen Burke.
All rights reserved. No part of this publication may be reproduced, stored in a retrieval system, or
transmitted, in any form or by any means, electronic, mechanical, photocopying, recording, or
otherwise, without the written prior permission of the author.

Note for Librarians: A cataloguing record for this book is available from Library
and Archives Canada at www.collectionscanada.ca/amicus/index-e.html

Printed in Victoria, BC, Canada.

ISBN: 978-1-4251-2216-4

*We at Trafford believe that it is the responsibility of us all, as both individuals and corporations,
to make choices that are environmentally and socially sound. You, in turn, are supporting this
responsible conduct each time you purchase a Trafford book, or make use of our publishing services.
To find out how you are helping, please visit www.trafford.com/responsiblepublishing.html*

*Our mission is to efficiently provide the world's finest, most comprehensive book publishing
service, enabling every author to experience success. To find out how to publish your book, your
way, and have it available worldwide, visit us online at www.trafford.com/10510*

www.trafford.com

North America & international
toll-free: 1 888 232 4444 (USA & Canada)
phone: 250 383 6864 ♦ fax: 250 383 6804 ♦ email: info@trafford.com

The United Kingdom & Europe
phone: +44 (0)1865 722 113 ♦ local rate: 0845 230 9601
facsimile: +44 (0)1865 722 868 ♦ email: info.uk@trafford.com

10 9 8 7 6 5 4 3 2

Acknowledgement

My thanks go to the following people without whose help this book might never have been printed:

My wife Sharon who has encouraged me throughout, tirelessly proof-reading rework after rework of my manuscripts, also my brother Joseph who translated many German documents for me, explained many German terms and created the 3D images of the *Graf Zeppelin* that appear in this book, while doing more than his own fair share of the proofreading.

Also giving much assistance were;
*   Hugh Alexander of the National Archive (Kew Gardens).
*   Kate Tildesley from the foreign documents section of the Naval Historical Branch.
*   Ian Proctor and Louise Oliver of the Imperial War Museum's photographic department.
*   Cmdr' Dr. Eng' Adam Olejnik from the Department of Diving Technology and Underwater Work at the Military Naval Academy in Gdynia, Poland.
*   Capt. of the 1st Rank I Shchetin, Head of the Central Naval Archives, Moscow.
*   Dave Ainsley, a respected friend.
*   Martina Caspers of the Bundesarchiv, Germany.
*   Nadine Wulz and Adela Trstenjak of Voith Schneider.

Last but by no means least my proofreader Louise Harnby, who did a marvellous job of proofing my manuscript.

The majority of images displayed in this book are done so under licence. I must offer my apologies to those copyright owners whom I have been unable to trace. If they can make themselves known to me I will be more than happy to discuss their required fee for the reproduction of their images or to withdraw their image from all subsequent editions of my book.

Contents

Glossary of Terms and Abbreviations

A.A.   Anti-Aircraft

AG (as in Kiel AG)   'Aktiengesellschaft' (a joint stock company)

AP   Armour Piercing

ASW   Anti-Submarine Warfare

Axis powers
(Oft. Referred to as 'the Axis') Mainly consisting of Germany, Italy and Japan (plus some smaller states such as Hungary and Rumania). These were the opponents to Great Britain and her allies in World War II

Bf (as in Bf 109)   Abbreviation for 'Bayerische Flugzeugwerke' a German aircraft manufacturer. The company's initials preceded the design number that was allocated to a new aircraft by the RLM. For example the Bf 109 (any letters following this number signifies a specific sub type). Bayerische would later change its name to Messerschmitt after Willi Messerschmitt, the Bf 109's chief designer. As a result of this change of name any future aircraft designed by the company would have the prefix 'Me' preceding the design number, resulting in the Bf 109 often (though incorrectly) being referred to as the Me 109.

CV	Carrier Vessel
Central Planning Committee	The body responsible for allocating steel
Dirigible	Airship
Flak	Abbreviation for 'Fliegerabwehrka-none', meaning 'anti aircraft gun'
Fliegerführer	Air force officer commanding a specific operation i.e. Fliegerführer Afrika
F.M.B.	Abbreviation for 'Funkmessbeobacht ungsgeräte' the German radar search receiver
HMS	Abbreviation for His Majesty's Ship – the prefix given to all Royal Navy vessels
IJN	Imperial Japanese Navy
JG (e.g. JG77)	Abbreviation for 'Jagdgeschwader' meaning 'Fighter group'
Ju (as in Ju87)	Abbreviation for 'Junker', the aircraft manufacturer. The first two letters of Junker's name preceded the design number that was allocated to a new aircraft by the RLM. For example the Ju 87 (any letters following this number signifies a specific sub type).
Kriegsmarine	German navy (between 1935 and 1945)
Luftwaffe	German air force
O.K.M.	Ober Kommando der Marine – The Kriegsmarine High Command (equivalent to "the Admiralty" in the Royal Navy)

Reich	Empire/Kingdom
Reichsmarschall	Herman Göring
RLM Reichsluftfahrtministerium	(Germany's State Ministry of Aviation)
Royal Navy	Great Britain's naval force
SKL	Abbreviation for 'Seekriegsleitung' meaning the Naval Warfare Staff. The SKL was subservient to the O.K.M.
Smoke-laying aircraft	Aircraft responsible for laying a smoke screen to hide a ship's movements.
Supermarina	The High Command of the 'Regia Marina' – Italy's Royal Navy.
Technische Amt	Technical office of the State Ministry of Aviation (RLM)
Third Reich	Third Kingdom/Empire. The First Reich was the Holy Roman Empire established by Emperor Charlemagne, the Second Reich was established with the founding of modern Germany in 1871 and ended with the abdication of Kaiser Wilhelm II shortly after World War I. Hitler believed he had established the Third Reich.
Tirpitz Principal	After Alfred von Tirpitz, the former Commander of the Kaiserliche Marine (the Imperial navy) and father of the modern German navy. Tirpitz had stipulated that, 'above all else a ship should stay afloat'
Trägergruppe	Carrier Group
USS	United States Ship

Introduction

I have tried at all times to keep this book as factual as possible. However, in preparing this book I have come across various documented inconsistencies on the subject of the *Graf Zeppelin*. For example, the length and width of the ship varies depending on whose work you read; I have largely based my statistics on those contained in the National Archive document 'ADMT 19137'. A first hand account, this document is a record of two separate visits to the carrier by Italian dignitaries. It provides information on the various statistics quoted to them by their German guides and gives an invaluable insight into the carrier. Unfortunately these figures at times appear to contradict the data presented by Wilhelm Hädeler (the designer of the *Graf Zeppelin*) in his book about the carrier, *Der Flugzeugträger*.

I feel that these apparent differences can and must be explained: though different neither figure is wrong, it is simply a matter of what you include (or exclude) in your measurement. Hädeler states the width of the carrier's flight deck to have been 30 metres – three metres wider than that declared by the Italians. However, what is not immediately clear is that Hädeler's measurement includes the trench-type gangway and other projections running along the side of the flight deck, where as the Italian measurement refers only to the runway.

Other variations such as flight deck length can be similarly explained away, this measurement being variable owing to the retractable catapults at the bow. When in their extended positions, the catapults projected beyond the edge of the flight deck thus increasing the measured length of the flight deck by several metres. The following table presents the dimensions of the carrier as stated by both Wilhelm Hädeler and the Italian commission:

Measured at	Hädeler's statistics	Statistics given to the Italian commission of 1941
LENGTH AT WATER LINE	250 m.	250 m
OVERALL LENGTH	262.5 m	272 m
WIDTH AT WATER LINE	27 m	27 m
OPERATIONAL DRAUGHT	7.6 m	6.1 m empty, 7.8 m when fully loaded (according to 1941 data)
SIDE HEIGHT	22.5 m	22.5 m
FLIGHT DECK LENGTH	244 m	239 m
FLIGHT DECK WIDTH	30 m	27 m (24 m corresponding to the superstructure)
UPPER HANGAR (LENGTH, WIDTH & HEIGHT)	185 m X 16 m X 5.9 m	185 m X 16 m X 5.9m
LOWER HANGAR (LENGTH, WIDTH & HEIGHT)	172 m X 16 m X 5.7 m	172 m X 16 m X 5.7 m
FLIGHT DECK HEIGHT OVER WATERLINE.	15.6 m	14.7 m

The only seemingly unexplainable variation is that of the overall length of the ship as claimed by the Italian commission in comparison with Wilhelm Hädeler's figures. Hädeler stated that the overall length of the ship was 262.5 metres after the addition of the 'Atlantic bow' (257.3 metres before the addition) the Italians apparently having been informed that it was 272 metres. Differing by some ten metres, a variation such as this can only really be explain away as a typing or clerical error on the 'Italian document' (ADMT 19137), and does not detract from the validity of the rest of the document.

Other inconsistencies I have come across from various sources indicate differing numbers of 20 mm weapons and even an alternative reason for the construction of the ship's counterpoise bulges, some sources claiming it was to counter the effects of adding more armour and a taller funnel, the Italians having been informed that it was the result of an error in her construction that caused her to list – an embarrassing admission and certainly not an excuse the Kriegsmarine would make up – making no comment about additional armour being added.

When encountering these and other contradictions I have chosen to trust in a little common sense, and whatever first hand accounts I have been able to draw on.

There is still much to be learned about the *Graf Zeppelin*, as much was lost in the chaos that understandably existed in Germany in the period after the war; many of the design drawings for this and other Kriegsmarine ships having been taken by the German Army and burned in advance of the Allied occupation.

Beginnings

Establishing a carrier class

December 8, 1938. With the launching ceremony complete, the first aircraft carrier of Germany's Kriegsmarine begins, imperceptibly at first, her journey towards the water.

Towering over 22 metres from keel to flight deck, and seemingly stretching back into infinity, she truly was a colossus that dwarfed the surrounding crowd. Even the Führer (Adolf Hitler) and other assembled dignitaries such as Herman Göring head of the Luftwaffe, occupying the raised podium beneath her bow from where the ceremony had been conducted, would have had to crane their necks to see the workers gathered high up on the flight deck immediately above the recently unfurled banners that had disclosed for the first time the carrier's name, *Graf Zeppelin*.

As is tradition, family members of anyone who had a vessel named in their honour would be invited to the launching ceremony. Thus, also there on the podium was Hella Von Brandstein-Zeppelin, daughter of the famous German airship builder, in whose honour the vessel had been named. In fact, it was Hella herself who had christened the carrier.

The roar erupting from the thousands of spectators assembled for this awesome spectacle drowns out the band's rendition of the national anthem 'Deutschland, Deutschland über alles…' as her bare hull, 250 metres long[1], begins with increasing momentum its journey to the water of the basin behind. Her new coat of arms proudly displayed on her bow glistens, the decoration of garlands, navy ensigns and pendants slung from bow to stern flutter wildly in the breeze.

As she enters the water for the first time, she survives her first real test, a test that all new ships must go through as the stern and mid-ships enters the water and the bow is still supported on the slipway, putting great strain on the new hull.

---

1   Waterline length

Graf Zeppelin begins her journey to the water. As the stern floats free of the slip, great strain is put on the hull - 8 December 1938. Bundesarchiv RM 25 Bild-27.

The keel of the *Graf Zeppelin* was laid on slipway Number One, as Flugzeugträger 'A' (Aircraft carrier 'A') on 28 December 1936 at the Deutsche werke shipyard, Kiel, which until a mere 20 days before had been home to the battleship *Gneisenau*, which famously went on to sink the British carrier *Glorious* and her escorts returning from Norway.

Two years earlier, *Gneisenau's* launch had started very similarly to that of the *Graf Zeppelin*. The band, crowd and dignitaries all present, the ship likewise emblazoned with flags, pendants and garlands all bellowing in the stiff breeze. The hull, until then known as construction 'E', was christened, and her name revealed to the world.

The ceremony complete, the battleship started her journey towards the water, but, as with all the best-laid plans, something went wrong. The drag chains that were supposed to stop her didn't. Reaching the water and floating free of the slipway for the first time, the motion of that great mass of steel did not glide to a braked halt, as was the plan, but instead carried on unchecked ploughing backwards through the water, driven by the momentum released on the slipway. The massive hulk of *Gneisenau* only stopped when it collided with the Hindenburg embankment opposite.

Lesson learnt, the second anniversary of that embarrassing day did not see a repeat performance. Even with a stiff breeze blowing, *Graf Zeppelin*, the biggest vessel ever built by Nazi Germany, offering over 4500 square metres of vertical steel walls to the wind, an area approximately equal to the sail area of the fully rigged cadet training ship *Prussen*, remained under control. Once the ceremony was complete, the newly named ship, still at this point merely an empty hulk, lacking any superstructure and without a funnel, was towed away to the equipping pier for the installation of her engine room machinery, guns and other equipment.

Graf Zeppelin is towed away to the equipping pier. Bundesarchiv Bild 146-1984-097-36

Designed by Naval Chief Architect Wilhelm Hädeler, the *Graf Zeppelin* was his and Germany's first attempt at an aircraft carrier, and would be a similar size to that of Great Britain's *Ark Royal* then still under construction. The original study was carried out by the 'K' office (Kriegsmarine Schiffs-

bau Büro[2]) from the end of 1933 to early 1934 (before Hitler had come to power), and was to be based on a request for a craft of approximately 20,000 tons (displacement), top speed of 33 knots and capable of carrying 50 – 60

Afloat but far from complete, construction of the carrier's superstructure begins. Bundesarchiv RM 25Bild-30

2   The 'K' office consisted of seven departments responsible for everything from ship design and construction, to installation work on shipyards and harbours.

aircraft. Armament would be based on light cruisers of the day, and internal watertight measures in line with the Tirpitz principal[3] resulted in 20 bulkheads dividing her hull, creating 21 watertight compartments.

Germany, like most other powers, unclear exactly what role these new vessels were going to play in the theatre of battle, wanted *Graf Zeppelin* to be capable of fighting her way out of an encounter with an enemy cruiser, and so they both armed and armoured her as a cruiser. Her armour actually surpassed in places that of their own *Admiral Hipper* class heavy cruisers, *Zeppelin*'s armoured deck being up to 60 mm thick in comparison with *Hipper*'s 50 mm (which narrowed in places to as little as 12 mm), her armoured belt at up to 100 mm being a full 20 mm thicker.

Originally planning to arm her with eight 203 mm guns in four casemates mounted on either side of the ship, a degree of sense would prevail and the calibre of these guns would be reduced to the smaller but faster-firing 150 mm gun. However, lack of clarity as to what role the aircraft carrier would serve in a conflict led to a further revision of her artillery, and the number of these heavy weapons would ultimately increase to 16 150 mm guns mounted in eight double casemates. For defence from attacking aircraft, ten 105 mm weapons were to be mounted in five twin fixtures, all on the starboard side of the flight deck, two forward of the bridge and three abaft the funnel. The light anti-aircraft (A.A.) armament was to consist of 11 automatically stabilised twin 37 mm installations, each equipped with a portable 1.25-metre rangefinder; these would be positioned five on each side of the ship mounted on platforms that projected outwards from the flight deck. A further installation mounted above the bow would have the capability of firing straight ahead or being brought to bear to either port or starboard. For close-quarter fighting, eight single 20 mm guns were intended to supplement the firepower of the 37 mm weapons, but it would not take long before the inadequacy of this arrangement was realised and plans were drawn up for the replacement of these single mounts with quadruple installations of these same guns.

As this was to be Germany's first aircraft carrier, Hädeler turned to other foreign navies for help in developing his ideas, as development abroad had been ongoing for a number of years. Hädeler's problem was that Germany had been left behind in the development of this most modern of weapons due to the terms of the Treaty of Versailles drawn up after World War I, the treaty denying Germany an air force and, amongst other things, aircraft carriers.

In his quest for information on designing aircraft carriers, Hädeler at first turned to Great Britain, one of the pioneers of this type of vessel. The Royal Navy had had an interest in carriers since before World War I. In fact by the start of World War I, Great Britain already had an operational carrier of sorts; by 1935 she was operating a fleet of carriers. It was to see

3   After Alfred von Tirpitz, the former Commander of the Kaiserliche Marine (the Imperial Navy) and father of the modern German Navy. Tirpitz had stipulated that, 'above all else a ship should stay afloat'.

one of these carriers, HMS *Furious*, that the representatives from the 'K' office visited Britain on a fact-finding mission during Navy Week, 1935. A subsequent visit to Japan to see His Imperial Majesty's aircraft carrier *Akagi* would however reap greater results, and the commission left with plans for such items as the central elevator and aircraft arrestor gear, but declined Japanese offers for a long-term study of their carriers. Though HMS *Furious* and the Imperial Japanese navy's (IJN) ship *Akagi* were used in the early stages of development, the *Graf Zeppelin* would be very different, far more sleek, her silhouette unique.

Designed with endurance in mind, every conceivable space on board her would be utilised, from the drying of clothes inside the exhaust casing to the stowing of stores inside her double bottom. She would sport her own operating theatre, isolation room, radiology room, dispensary, photography room and enough food for eight weeks at sea, fresh water being produced by three onboard evaporators.

To ensure her sustained performance, her turbines could be disengaged from the turning propeller shafts even at speed, allowing work to be carried out on the turbines, and then re-engaged by synchronising the revolutions with that of the idling shaft. Conversely, when stationary, the turbines could be disengaged from the propeller shafts to allow the turbines to be put through their paces.[4]

In 1937, Hitler informed Grand Admiral Erich Raeder, Commander-in-Chief of the Ober Kommando der Marine[5] (O.K.M.) that war with Great Britain was inevitable. This resulted in the creation of the 'Z' plan, a plan for the rapid expansion of the Kriegsmarine that would include the creation of a fleet of four aircraft carriers. The genesis of this carrier fleet had begun the year before with the laying of keel 'A' (*Graf Zeppelin*), which it had been intended to follow in late 1938 (shortly before the launch of keel 'A') by keel 'B' at the Krupp Germania shipyard also in Kiel.

Though contracts for the laying of both keels had been agreed at the same time (16 November, 1935), the delay between the two was partly out of necessity (the only suitable slipway at Krupps was occupied by the heavy cruiser *Prinz Eugen*) and partly to give the inevitable opportunities to learn from the construction of carrier 'A'.

Legend has it that carrier 'B' was to be named *Peter Straßer* after the famous World War I airship pilot and classmate of Grand Admiral Raeder killed on a bombing mission over Britain, but due to the German policy of not assigning a name to a ship until it is launched we shall never know. Though the keel for carrier 'B' was laid, the gathering momentum of the war that had begun in September of 1939 would see it broken up in early 1940, as both the steel and the slipway were needed for other more pressing wartime matters, such as U-boat construction.

Some of the equipment that had been destined for carrier 'B' such as

4   National Archive document: ADMT 19137

5   The Kriegsmarine High Command

the 16 boilers (12 built by Deutsche Werke, and 4 by Germaniawerft) intended for installation in the vessel, had already been completed, and so they were sent to various parts of Germany, such as:

2 – Brückner Karnis, Dresden.

2 – to a power station at Gotenhafen.

4 – Installed in test house at Germaniawerft.

2 – at Blohm & Voss, Hamburg.

2 – at Wumag-Gorlitz.[6]

Other items, such as catapults that had been intended for the second carrier, would later be earmarked for a life in the Mediterranean, offered to Germany's Italian ally to aid with their own carrier *Aquila*.

The impromptu start to the war had sounded the death knell for Germany's carrier fleet; only the *Graf Zeppelin* would remain, the sole survivor from the Kriegsmarine planned carrier force. She would be the last steamship launched at Kiel before the yard switched exclusively to U-boat construction.

---

6 Extracted from 'La Mont Boilers in Germany', BIOS final report number 382. (Imperial War Museum collection, Duxford).

Carrier Development

THE GENESIS OF THE CARRIER AGE AND ITS ROLE IN MODERN WARFARE

By June 1913 the British cruiser HMS *Hermes* had been converted to take a wheeled launching platform and at first she operated two seaplanes; by the time 'The Great War' had begun in October 1914 she carried ten. But *Hermes*'s war career was short-lived and unspectacular: on the evening of 30 October 1914 she was torpedoed and sunk by the submarine *U27*. The value of such a radical vessel as *Hermes* being apparent to someone at the Admiralty, a replacement for her was quickly ordered, a merchant ship being fitted out with similar launching apparatus to that of the *Hermes*. This ship, HMS *Ark Royal*, her name of great provenance in the Royal Navy, like all subsequent ships to bear this name would prove a valuable asset in the years ahead. *Ark Royal*, with a name that went back to 1588 and the Spanish Armada, would be 350 feet long, weighed 7450 tons and could travel at 11 knots. She could carry six two-seater seaplanes and two single-seat landplanes. Like all carriers since, she projected British aircraft capability to distant conflicts, even following the war across to the Dardanelles, where on 5 March 1915 the crew of one of her Sopwith seaplanes had a miraculous escape, when, having climbed to 3000 feet to direct gunfire on a Turkish fort, the aircraft's propeller fell off and they plunged into the sea.

Early in the war, the Royal Navy commandeered a number of fast cross-channel steamers and converted them into seaplane carriers. In December 1914 the converted steamers *Engadine*, *Empress* and *Riviera* converged 12 miles north of Heligoland, and proceeded to hoist their seaplanes onto the water. In all, seven planes took off, their target being the Zeppelin (dirigible[7]) sheds at Cuxhaven. Though none of the aeroplanes found the sheds and four were forced to ditch in the sea (three of the crews being picked up by a friendly submarine, the fourth being captured by a Dutch trawler), the aircraft that returned to their ships that day were able

---

7   Airships

to give invaluable information about German-held harbours and the ships moored in them.

It was from *Engadine*, on 31 May 1916 during the battle of Jutland, that a Short 184 seaplane was launched, making history as it made the first ever air reconnaissance of a fleet in action. Planning to report on the position of three German light cruisers, the mission was cut short when the aircraft's engine failed, but gave some indication of the possibilities of these fragile aircraft. Another converted steamer, HMS *Ben My Chree* had the honour of launching the first aircraft to carry out a successful aerial torpedo strike, sinking a German ship.

It was, however, obvious that seaplanes were not the way ahead; it took 20 minutes just to launch and get a seaplane into the air, which would only be able to land back on the water for recovery in calm weather. The Royal Navy experimented with various ideas, from turret-launch systems, where aircraft were carried over and catapulted from the turret of a warship, to a system where an aircraft was towed out to sea behind a ship on a floating platform that would allow the launch of either sea or landplanes. This gave them the ability to serve as anti-submarine aircraft, their range being greatly increased by their free ride out to sea.

The increased performance of land-based aircraft over seaplanes prompted experiments to launch an aircraft from the deck of a ship, the newly completed HMS *Furious* being selected for these trials. *Furious* was one of three new ships planned as fast (at the cost of armour), heavily armed cruisers with a shallow draught (originally designed to operate in the Baltic, where it was hoped 1,000,000 German soldiers could be diverted from the Western Front to the Baltic coast), all of which would eventually be converted to operate aircraft. Initially fitted with a short take-off platform over the bow that was 50 feet wide and 228 feet long, experiments for the landing of aircraft onto this deck would soon follow. On 2 August 1917 with HMS *Furious* heading into a stiff breeze, a Sopwith Pup piloted by Squadron Commander E. H. Dunning landed on her forward deck. With a remarkable piece of flying Dunning came in alongside *Furious*, passing her amidships' central superstructure at just above landing speed, and at the last moment, with a gentle sideslip, touched down onto her deck. Two days later, in a repeat of the exercise, a tyre burst on touchdown and the plane went over the side killing Dunning.

The late Squadron Commander's legacy had been to demonstrate that landings on deck, and whilst underway, were indeed possible, and so the addition of a 'landing-on' platform aft of the superstructure to safely facilitate this was a logical progression. However, turbulence created by the superstructure made landing so dangerous it had to be stopped until further refits in 1925 saw *Furious* emerging with her superstructure removed, a full-length flight deck 576 feet long, and, below that, a lower 'flying-off' deck from which aircraft could take off directly from their below-deck hangers, a feature the Japanese would copy in their carriers *Akagi* and *Kaga*.

After Dunning's success in 1917, what is considered the world's first true aircraft carrier was built. Starting life in a British shipyard as the Italian liner *Conte Rosso*, its construction would be halted by World War I and the necessity to focus Britain's industry on meeting the needs of a country at war. In 1916, the same month that HMS *Furious* was launched, the half-finished liner's construction began again. She would be completed not as a liner but as the 14,450 ton HMS *Argus* (*Argus*: a mythical beast with many eyes). With lessons learned from the conversion of HMS *Furious*, plans for a bow launching platform, central superstructure and aft-landing platform would be replaced to give her an unimpeded flight deck 558 feet long by 60 feet wide from which aircraft could both take off and land. In an attempt to resolve command problems for the bridge staff (a totally flat deck required the bridge to be tucked away under the deck and the lack of standing radio masts caused communication problems) she would trial a tiny superstructure, all on the starboard side, creating the world's first island carrier and resolving many of the aircraft control and steering problems. She would be the prototype for all modern carriers. Launched in December 1917 and commissioned in September 1918 a mere two months before the end of the war, she was too late to see any action. *Argus* spent the next ten years being used to develop aircraft carrier technique, and, amongst other things, training pilots in the art of landing on a carrier. The lessons learned on her would be incorporated into future carriers and would ultimately influence the design of a new HMS *Hermes* (so named after the mythical *Hermes* the winged messenger). Begun in 1917, *Hermes*'s keel would be the first in the world to be laid for a ship designed and built as a carrier but, due to numerous delays, she was not completed until 1924.

Delays in the initial completion of *Argus* meant Admiral Beatty's 1918 plan to strike at the German fleet in its harbours, with massed torpedo carrying aircraft, would not come to fruition and the world would have to wait another 22 years for such a demonstration of carrier-borne might, when on 11 November 1940 aircraft from HMS *Illustrious* attacked the Italian harbour of Taranto sinking three battleships including the new *Littorio* and damaging several other ships and harbour facilities. The 21 Fairy Swordfish deployed that night from HMS *Illustrious* were slow, outdated biplanes, known affectionately as 'old string bags', but at a stroke they would change the balance of sea power in the Mediterranean.

In the early 1930s HMS *Argus* would be laid up only to be recalled again as a training ship, and, with the coming of another war with Germany, she would see her first action. Though by now obsolete, desperate times require desperate measures, and these early years were desperate. She would see action delivering aircraft to Gibraltar and Malta, on the Arctic convoys, and was involved in the North Africa landings. From 1943 *Argus* was used once again as a training ship in home waters. Paid off in December 1944, she would be used as an accommodation ship until 1945, prior to scrapping in 1947.

Development of carriers went on independently around the world, Japan taking a lead by being the first nation to complete a keel-up carrier (i.e. a ship designed and built from the keel up as a carrier) with the IJN *Hosho*. *Hosho* had been commissioned in 1922 (three years after her keel was laid) and by the time Japan attacked Pearl Harbour in December of 1941, she would have the biggest carrier fleet in the Pacific with nine carriers in service, compared with the USA's seven.

America had been greatly influenced by the experiences of Great Britain in operating its aircraft carriers during World War I, when aircraft had proven invaluable in anti-submarine warfare (ASW). Before the end of the war aircraft were flying off the decks of Britain's ships and trials with aircraft carriers that could not only launch but also receive aircraft back on deck were underway. Ships designated as carriers were the way ahead. Indeed, Britain was leading the way, having by the end of the Great War in 1918 three operating carriers, two training carriers and two under construction.

The USA had been an early pioneer in the development of carriers, being the first to land an aircraft onto a ship's deck, the feat being credited to Eugene Ely who landed on a platform on the armoured cruiser USS *Pennsylvania* in January 1911 (he made the first take-off from a ship two months previously). Slow to develop this new alliance of aircraft and naval vessel, between Ely's landing on the *Pennsylvania* and the commissioning of America's first carrier, eleven years would pass. In the meantime, they would experiment with turret-launched aircraft as the British had done, catapulting aircraft from launching platforms mounted over gun turrets. However, shortcomings with such systems were demonstrated on board the USS *Huntington*, when during the firing of a practice salvo her aircraft were destroyed by the concussion of her own guns.

It fell to the most unglamorous of vessels, a naval collier named *Jupiter*, entering Norfolk Navy Yard in March 1920 and being re-designated 'CV' (carrier vessel) to indicate the start of America's carrier fleet. *Jupiter* would be commissioned two years later as the USS *Langley* (CV1) and for the next five years *Langley* would be the sole carrier of the US Navy. *Langley's* success however would ensure the completion of CV's 2 and 3 the USS *Lexington* and *Saratoga*.

Langley would have an obstruction-free flight deck just like Great Britain's first carriers. The flight deck would be 534 feet long and 64 feet wide. On subsequent US carriers, as would be the trend set by HMS *Argus* and followed on a grander scale on board HMS *Hermes*, the obstruction-free deck would be replaced by an island type superstructure on the starboard side; starboard was selected for the island's location as it provided a better view of buoy markers in narrow channels, apparently also facilitating left-hand turns, which the aircraft pilots preferred owing to the torque of the turning propeller.

Japan's dramatic entry into the war with America would demonstrate her aircraft carrier capability, proving that Lieutenant Commander McDonnel, a visionary from 20 years before, was right to worry that 'a fleet of carriers could attack a place like Hawaii'. On 7 December 1941, the US Navy's anchorage on Hawaii, Pearl Harbour was indeed attacked, decimating the battleships of her Pacific fleet anchored on 'Battleship Row'. In terms of hardware the US got off lightly at Pearl Harbour, with the Pacific Fleet's aircraft carriers all being at sea and thus escaping a crushing defeat that would have taken them years to recover from. The Japanese would have to wait another five months after Pearl Harbour to get the opportunity to confront their American carrier counterparts, carriers from both fleets meeting for the first time in the Battle of the Coral Sea. Separated by 175 miles, for the first time in naval history a battle ensued in which surface ships from neither fleet would set eyes on each other. Fought far beyond the range of the big guns of either fleet's battleships, even the recently completed monstrous white elephant that was the Japanese super battleship *Yamato* with her 18-inch guns and their 40 km range, had she been present, would have contributed little. Relegated to the role of a floating anti-aircraft battery, *Yamato* would have been just another target for the American aircraft.

The Battle of the Coral Sea was a victory for the US Navy with one Japanese carrier sinking (the small escort carrier *Shoho*) and two major carriers, the *Shokaku* and *Zuikaku*, being damaged, one severely, for the loss of CV2, the USS *Lexington* and damage to the USS *Yorktown* (CV5). Though the US in the loss of the *Lady Lex* had lost a major vessel against one small Japanese carrier, the damage to the two large Japanese carriers would ensure they would not be present at the Battle of Midway a week later. Also Japan's mistaken belief that the USS *Yorktown* had sunk would lead them to believe the United States had fewer major ships than they really had. The Battle of the Coral Sea was the first real victory against the Japanese and the psychological advantage needed by the United States. Importantly, the US had denied Japan the victory it needed in order to occupy Papua New Guinea's Port Moresby, from where land-based aircraft would have secured the air superiority needed to bomb mainland Australia.

On the other side of the world, though the results of Midway would not be known for some time, Kriegsmarine officers would begin to regret more than ever their lack of an operational aircraft carrier, a situation that must have become harder to comprehend as time went on, especially when they already had an aircraft carrier afloat and 85 per cent complete. Surely the aircraft carrier had proven its power and its worth?

Birth of a Leviathan

THE FALL AND RISE OF A NATION

'Murdered with cold calculation': that was how the Reich Stadt's Foreign Office Minister Count Brockdorff-Rantzau speaking in May 1919 at the Versailles peace conference described the death of hundreds of thousands of Germans from hunger, resulting from the continuation of the blockade of an impotent Germany's ports that prevented the much-needed food and materials arriving after the November eleventh ceasefire of 1918.

In a state of economic collapse, on the verge of Communist revolution, and with much of the Imperial navy's High Seas fleet disarmed and interned way up north at the outer limits of the British Isles in the Royal Navy base of Scapa Flow, Germany had no choice but to sign the Treaty of Versailles (the diktat as it was commonly referred to in Germany). The treaty consisted of 440 Articles covering everything from aeroplanes to child employment legislation. It would make Germany admit full responsibility for the war. Taking on much of the vast amount of resulting debt (plus interest), she would have to hand over literally several hundred thousand farm and working animals, rail rolling stock and engines by the thousands. Her merchant navy would be all but disbanded by the handing over of ships from her fleet in reparations for allied merchant ships lost in action throughout the war. Agricultural machinery, and many other basics needed to rebuild the country, were taken. Germany's once proud navy would be decimated, left as a mere shadow of its former self, the treaty dictating that:

ARTICLE 181.

After the expiration of a period of two months from the coming into force of the present Treaty the German naval forces in commission must not exceed:

6 battleships of the Deutschland or Lothringen type, 6 light cruisers, 12 destroyers, 12 torpedo boats, or an equal number of ships con-

structed to replace them as provided in Article 190.

No submarines are to be included.

ARTICLE 190.

Germany is forbidden to construct or acquire any warships other than those intended to replace the units in commission provided for in Article l81 of the present Treaty.

The warships intended for replacement purposes as above shall not exceed the following displacement:

Armoured ships 10,000 tons
Light cruisers 6,000 tons
Destroyers 800 tons
Torpedo boats 200 tons

Except where a ship has been lost, units of the different classes shall only be replaced at the end of a period of twenty years in the case of battleships and cruisers, and fifteen years in the case of destroyers and torpedo boats, counting from the launching of the ship.

As far as Great Britain and her allies were concerned, Germany, suitably dealt with in the Treaty of Versailles, had no business in future dealings on armament. Germany would not be invited to Washington for the conference of late 1921 where the leading world powers would agree a treaty limiting the size of future warships, a futile attempt to avoid another arms race which most could ill afford. The signatories at 'the Washington conference' agreed that:

WASHINGTON, NOVEMBER 12 1921-FEBRUARY 6, 1922.

Treaty Between the United States of America, the British Empire, France, Italy, and Japan, Signed at Washington, February 6, 1922. [41]

No vessel of war exceeding 10,000 tonnes (10,160 Imperial tons) standard displacement, other than a capital ship or aircraft carrier, shall be acquired by, or constructed by, for, or within the jurisdiction of, any of the Contracting Powers. Vessels not specifically built as fighting ships nor taken in time of peace under government control for fighting purposes, which are employed on fleet duties or as troop transports or in some other way for the purpose of assisting in the prosecution of hostilities otherwise than as fighting ships, shall not be within the limitations of this Article.

Article XII

No vessel of war of any of the Contracting Powers, hereafter laid down, other than a capital ship, shall carry a gun with a calibre in excess of 8 inches (203 millimetres).

Unwittingly, the Washington Treaty (1922) signatories gave the Reichsmarine (as the Imperial navy was by now known) the lead in fire-power over their own cruisers. This lead came about due to the Washington Treaty determining shipping tonnage in metric tonnes and deeming future cruisers of the signatory powers to be limited to 10,000 metric tonnes and a maximum calibre gun of 8 inches. Germany, not included in the Washington Treaty, was still bound by the Treaty of Versailles, which allowed her to replace her elderly battleships with vessels of 10,000 imperial tons, armed with 11-inch guns. Quick to notice the similarity in tonnage of a 'Washington cruiser' as compared with their own battleships, Germany took the opportunity to quietly replace their allocation of 10,000 imperial tons with the slightly larger 10,000 metric tonnes.[8] By the end of the decade Germany's engineers would be utilising this extra tonnage in the design of the 'Pocket battleships', constructing ships the same size as the so-called 'Washington cruisers' but armed with the significantly larger 11-inch (280 mm) gun.

German development of the now illegal U-boats as with the similarly illegal aircraft continued abroad, with research into submarines after 1918 continuing in Holland at 'Ingenieurskantoor voor Scheepsbouw'[9] (a cover name for what was in reality a German research laboratory operating there until Hitler came to power in 1933 and brought the 'research' back to Germany). Between the wars the 'Dutch' made U-boats for Finnish, Turkish and Spanish navies, work that kept Germany's stealth weapon of the Great War abreast of technology.

As the Treaty of Versailles continued to tighten its grip on the German economy, the German Mark plummeted in value and by 1923 there was an incredible 600,000 Marks to the Pound (Sterling). This same year the NSDAP (National Socialist German Workers Party), founded three years previously out of the ashes and turmoil that followed 1918 (the NSDAP would ultimately be known as the Nazi party) was banned after attempting to overthrow the Bavarian government by force.

Through this post-war era, Germany would try to rebuild herself, and the armed forces would not be left out. By January 1925 Germany's first major warship since the Great War, the light cruiser *Emden*, was launched followed in 1928 by the *Köln*, Germany's first new design of warship since the Great War. Three years later the Reichsmarine possessed the revolutionary pocket battleship *Deutschland*, with a second 'Pocket' being commissioned later that same year. The *Deutschland*'s specifications would be arrived at after discussion about new battleships led the Reichsmarine to discuss several design options including a monitor design. Ultimately they would settle on the 280 mm guns, 100 mm armour and 26 knots of the *Deutschland*.

The *Deutschland* would herald a new era in marine construction, and would see the Reichsmarine start to claw back some of the disadvan-

8   10,000 metric tons is equivalent to 10,160 Imperial tons.

9   Evaluation report No.76, 8 June 1945 (Imperial War Museum collection, Duxford).

tages forced upon it by the Versailles diktat. Technological advances such as the development by the steel giant Krupp of two new types of steel, Wotan hard (capable of deflecting projectiles) and Wotan soft (capable of absorbing them) both of which could be welded together without losing their properties, were a major breakthrough in warship design. This new development would allow ships to be constructed out of armoured plate rather than hanging armour onto the side of the hull as had been the practice around the world up until this point. Diesel technology would allow these new ships greater range (20,000 nautical miles) and reduce the need for refuelling at sea. The pocket battleships could outgun their opposite numbers in service with foreign navies (the term 'pocket battle-ship' was a reference to the great firepower, range and armoured protec-tion of these exceptionally powerful armoured cruisers), whose ships, thanks to the Washington Treaty of 1922, only possessed 8-inch guns (203 mm), and, at the time of their creation, the 'pockets' could outrun almost any vessel they could not outgun.

Other developments would come from the merchant marine. In June 1927 the keel of the liner *Bremen* was laid, and in a publication of the day contemporary critics would comment, 'an increased knowledge of stream-lining, made her designers decide to give her a bulb-shaped stem below the waterline, in place of the hitherto universally used fine stem. This innova-tion gave the ship buoyancy forward and also prevented her from plung-ing in rough seas and lifting her propellers.'[10] This 'bulb-shaped stem', the so-called 'Taylor pear', would be included in the construction of Germany's warships, the carrier *Graf Zeppelin* included. The benefits of having a more stable battleship for the accuracy of her gunnery, or a floating airstrip that pitches a little less, being obvious.

The footings for naval aircraft and fliers had already been established back in 1928 with the establishment under Captain Zander of a naval air arm. The first navy fliers bypassed the Treaty of Versailles ban on German military aircraft with the creation of 'Air Services Incorporated' which they gained by arguing the need for some aircraft so that the navy could practice firing its anti-aircraft guns at towed targets. With the passing of time there were inevitable circumventions of the Treaty; Admiral Raeder's 1932 re-placement plan for the fleet would include the hitherto illegal U-boats and naval aviation squadrons. In this same year, Deutsche werke, Kiel, had built an effective catapult for shipboard use and the navy was testing an aerial torpedo at the Eckernförde Torpedo experimental institute. Also by 1932 the navy had prototypes for both a multi-purpose aeroplane for bombing, mining and dropping torpedoes and a pursuit fighter.

Germany's naval aviation squadrons would still be in their infancy when, in 1933, Hitler became Chancellor, bringing with him the new German Air Force (headed by Hermann Göring), raising the question of whether the navy needed a separate air force at all. It did not take long

---

10   Shipping Wonders of the World Part 6 pg184

before Göring and Raeder clashed over naval flying with Göring insisting that 'everything that flies belongs to us!' Göring and Raeder would never see eye to eye; they would clash repeatedly in the coming years, a situation that continued with Raeder's eventual successor to the role of Grand Admiral, Karl Dönitz.

In August 1934 President von Hindenburg died. Immediately all branches of the armed forces swore a new oath of allegiance, this time not to the Fatherland but to Adolf Hitler as 'Supreme Commander' of the armed forces. In 1935 Hitler met with Great Britain and France to discuss armaments, with a plan that he had first outlined to Raeder early in 1933, shortly after he (Hitler) had become Chancellor. The plan intended for Germany to increase the size of her naval forces, by establishing a ratio of 3:1 with Great Britain on surface ships (commonwealth fleet included), with the right to build up to parity in submarines (though initially the total in submarines would only be 45 per cent of British vessels). This naval agreement was supposed to demonstrate to Great Britain that Germany was not a threat, and in a world where the specter of an unaffordable arms race with Japan (amongst others) was by now looming, would be gratefully accepted by Britain. No doubt, Hitler's plan to negotiate this new naval treaty with Great Britain was behind his lack of willingness to add a third turret in 1934 for the two battleships already authorised under the 1934 budget (*Scharnhorst* and *Gneisenau*).

Japan, growing in displeasure with the Washington and London naval agreements, both of which limited the size of her Imperial fleet so as to tip the power balance in favour of the US and Great Britain, had given the required two years notice on 29 December 1934 to quit both. Japan's growing military ambitions could only help Hitler in his negotiations with Great Britain. Hitler's confidence increasing, on 16 March 1935 he rejected the Treaty of Versailles and two months later, renamed the Reichsmarine the Kriegsmarine (literally meaning 'War navy'). Both of these acts would have given the impression to the British that Germany intended to expand its naval forces. Couple this with the global depression and the Japanese announcement of their intention to expand, Great Britain would be only too pleased to have an agreement that would control Germany's naval construction.

With the signing of the Anglo – German naval agreement, the Kriegsmarine would waste no time in announcing the construction of its new fleet of battleships, battle cruisers, destroyers and the hitherto illegal submarines. At the same time, plans were also made for the utilisation of Germany's allowance for aircraft carrier construction. Thanks to the study presented by the 'K' office the year before defining the desired speed, armour, armament, and aircraft capacity of their carriers, the Kriegsmarine already knew what it wanted from these vessels; it also knew it could have two of them each approximating to

20,000 tons. With the prospect of building a carrier now reality, the 'K' office visited Britain's HMS *Furious* being displayed during Navy Week for some inspiration, but would gain little from this early carrier. They would be more successful in their visit to Japan and the carrier *Akagi*, returning with plans for elevators and aircraft arrestors essential for flight-deck operations.

By November 16 of this same year, Deutsche werke, Kiel AG would receive the contract for the construction of Germany's first aircraft carrier, which in time would become the *Graf Zeppelin*. Costing 92.7 million Reichsmark, she would be powered by 16 La Mont oil-fired water pipe boilers each supplying steam to one of her four Brown Boveri turbines. In its entirety (boilers, engines, associated equipment, propellers and shafts etc. included) her engine room machinery would weigh an incredible 3560 tons, but would provide more horsepower than any other in the German fleet. Needing just one hour to raise steam (in reality half an hour was all that was needed to raise steam, but the turbines needed a full hour of heating before they were ready for operation), she would be able to accelerate from a standing start up to 20 knots in just two minutes.

Each of *Graf Zeppelin*'s 900 m³ boiler rooms would house four boilers each capable of producing 60 tons of steam per hour. Superheated to 450°C and at a working pressure of 70 bar,[11] steam from each boiler room fed one of the four Brown Boveri turbines, each consisting of a high-pressure turbine which was also the cruising turbine, a medium-pressure and a low-pressure turbine coupled to the propeller shaft via a reduction gear. The turbines themselves were housed in three separate compartments running longitudinally through the ship, with the smallest, the 800 m³ Turbine Room One, farthest aft feeding the port inner propeller. Forward of this and taking advantage of the widening form of the hull was the 1300 m³ starboard propellers turbine room, and forward of this the largest of the three turbine rooms which fed the two outer propeller shafts and occupied 1450 m³.

To ensure the exceptional power needed for carrier operations, each turbine was capable of producing up to 50,000 hp giving a total of 200,000 hp available to rotate the four 4.4-metre diameter props at up to 300 rpm allowing for a cruising speed of 32 knots (some reports claim up to 35 knots). Even at speed, any turbine could be disengaged from the spinning propeller shaft allowing work to be carried out on the necessary turbine, and, by matching the revolutions of the idling shaft, re-engaged at any time.[12]

---

11 Extracted from 'La Mont Boilers in Germany' Bios Final Report No. 382 (Imperial War Museum collection, Duxford).

12 The turbines work on a reduction gear connected by a coupling to the shaft of the propeller. These couplings are of the comb type ('a pettine') and can be worked even when the ship is in port, up to a speed of 18 knots by synchronising the revolutions of the turbines with those of the propeller shaft, while it is turning loose. (National Archive document ADMT 19137)

Completed up to the armoured deck. The two gapping holes nearest the camera are the cavities which would later allow for the insertion of the Graf Zeppelin's boilers. Bundesarchiv RM 25 Bild-09

With a variety of boilers available, the choice of the La Mont boiler was not a random decision. Automated control of the addition of air, water and fuel oil into the boiler completely eliminated the production of smoke, allowing for the quick 'raising of steam' and variations of speed.[13] The La Mont boiler was considered more flexible in design with regards to the amount and shape of space available, in comparison to the equally reliable, though easier to construct, maintain and operate Deschimag Wagner boiler system (that was the favoured arrangement towards the end of the war due to its simplicity and ability to be operated by less-experienced personnel). With all the associated exhaust pipe work from the boilers heading over to the carrier's starboard mounted funnel, the limited height imposed by this would again have favoured the La Mont boiler system in what was de- scribed as an 'extremely congested' boiler room by Allied inspectors shortly after the end of the war. Touring the recently occupied Germania Werft in 1945, the inspectors had visited a replica of the aircraft carrier's boiler room, installed exactly as if on board a carrier. It was constructed from boilers originally intended for the scrapped carrier 'B' and was being used as a turbine test house.[14]

The installation of high-pressure, high-temperature turbines on the most modern ships of the German fleet had been somewhat of a gamble. Grand Admiral Erich Raeder was very aware that the pocket battleships had lost much of the appeal they once had; it was no longer the case that they could outrun what they could not outgun. The other great navies of the world were now building fast, heavily armoured and heavily armed

13 National Archive document: ADMT 19137

14 Taken from BIOS report Nos 382 & 1333 (Imperial War Museum).

battleships that could out-perform their German 'pocket' counterparts in all but cruising range. If the Kriegsmarine was to stay ahead of the game, an educated gamble was required. A decision had to be made as to what type of power plant to install on the new ships *Scharnhorst* and *Gneisenau*, and recent developments in high-temperature, high-pressure steam installations for shore-based industrial plant were looking very promising. Unfortunately it would not be possible to trial these new engines, as in Raeder's words, '... although continuing development of the high temperature, high pressure, steam power plant was a high priority project at the MAN plant, the new engines had not yet proved up to the high speed and high performance required for the new battleships. Waiting to develop them further would have caused unacceptable delay in the completion of our new battleships, cruisers and destroyers. I had to decide at once. My decision was to take the risk and go straight to the turbine engine with the new high temperature high pressure steam.' Though the engines were tested on shore installations before being installed on smaller ships such as minesweepers and destroyers, they would still not be running consistently at a high level of performance when hostilities began in 1939, many problems having to be smoothed out during the war. It was clear to Raeder 'from the very beginning, though, that despite the advantages in higher speed, less weight, and smaller space requirements, the new power plants would never give the long cruising radius of the older diesel with its low rate of fuel consumption.'[15] The lack of range would be a real problem for the Kriegsmarine when hostilities against Great Britain began. Boxed in from the all important Atlantic with few allies in the world, once her ships had broken out into the Atlantic, if they were to stay out for any length of time, the options for refueling were severely limited. Her fleet would be dependent on a network of auxiliary supply ships for both refueling and rearming at sea, or forced to return to German homeports running the gauntlet of the British Isles.

Initially calculated to displace 19,700 tons, design alterations to carrier 'A' during construction meant this figure increased to 22,000 tons, which would equate to approximately 30,000 tons once loaded with aircraft, fuel, munitions and other stores necessary for a mission. Ultimately measuring 250 metres from bow to stern (at the waterline), 262.5 metres overall,[16] her flight deck would stand 22.5 metres above her keel, and be 239 meters long and 27 metres wide (narrowing to 24 meters at the superstructure). It would accommodate two compressed air catapults capable of launching aircraft of up

---

15 'As regards efficiency, the best consumption they had aimed at was 300 grams of oil per H.P. hour and this was practically achieved in the case of the *GRAF ZEPPELIN*. About 350 grams was the normal best figure obtained afloat by the smaller ships.' Taken from '*La Mont Boilers in Germany*' *BIOS final report number 382*. (Imperial War Museum collection, Duxford)

16 The Italian commission who visited the ship in 1941 quotes the overall length as 272m, but Hädeler's own figures put this at 262.5m. Though I have generally quoted the Italian commissions figures, on balance one would have to presume Hädeler's figure for overall length to be correct as an additional 22m of ship extending beyond that of the 250m waterline measurement as suggested by the Italians seems excessive.

Taken before her launch, this picture clearly demonstrates the support structure of the flight deck. The two square holes where casemates, each housing twin 150 mm guns, would later be installed can be seen. Bundesarchiv Bild 146-1982-145-29A

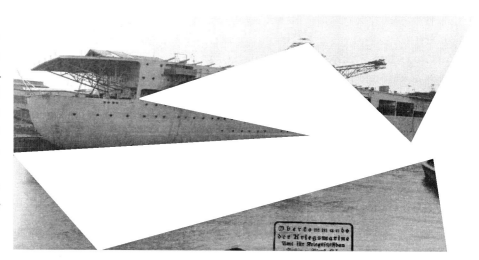

Looking from the stern, the supporting structure of the flight deck is visible. Here we see the aft casemate enclosure projecting out from the side of the ship, another two, twin 150 mm casemates were intended to be located here. Bundesarchiv RM 25 Bild-28

to five tons at a speed of 133 kmh (or a smaller 2.6 ton aircraft at 140 kmh) mounted at the bows. The steel flight deck would be covered in wood and supported on a combination of internal longitudinal bulkheads of the hangar below and tubular supports at the ship's extremities (sides, bow and stern).

Once operational she would draw approximately 7.8 metres but her flight deck would tower another 14.7 metres above the waterline. With such a vast amount of steel projecting above the waterline she would present a significant 'sail area' which would make her difficult to manoeuvre at slow speeds and in confined waters such as the Kiel Canal via which she would sail to access the North Sea. To counter the effects of the wind on this 'sail area', two retractable thrusters were situated towards the bows. Manufactured by Voith Schneider, this ingenious device was controlled from the bridge and could be lowered from its housing in the base of the hull at speeds of up to 12 knots providing thrust in any direction.

There were two inherent weak points in the design of the carrier: hangar decks that ran one above the other unobstructed on both 'C' and 'D' decks for much the length of the ship; and the three gapping holes in the flight deck, voids that would be filled by the raised elevators. These giant elevators, platforms measuring 14 metres by 13 metres, were necessary to transport aircraft from the hangars to the flight deck, but resulted in the flight deck, as a resisting structure and thus inseparably linked to the strength of the vessel, being twice as thick as would otherwise be necessary. It was constructed of hardened, high-resistance steel that possessed anti-splinter capabilities and was capable of absorbing a 20 ton impact (i.e. four times the weight of the planned heaviest aircraft, the Ju 87s) but was not armoured. Only the 60 mm-thick deck that formed the floor of the lower hangar was armoured, so as to protect the engine rooms, boiler rooms, magazines, and other vital areas of the ship.

The magazines below the armoured deck were intended by 1942 to consist of both 250 lb and 500 lb bombs in a forward magazine and typically 66 torpedoes and 48 mines at the stern, not to mention the munitions for the onboard guns and the 69,000 rounds of ammunition for her aircraft, all of which would be held in positive atmosphere magazines – a precaution that would negate the need for spark arrestors in this volatile part of the ship.[17] A variety of hoists situated beneath the relevant gun transported ammunition from the magazines located below the relative safety of the armoured deck to the gun emplacements above. Those hoists that served the 150 mm naval guns would have to be deflected to pass outside of the hangar decks that were located immediately above the magazines but the bombs for the aircraft, stored in the forward stowage area would be hoisted directly to the relevant hangar deck where they would be loaded onto the aircraft. The torpedoes, being a complicated weapon, would be hoisted directly from the stern stowage area into the torpedo workshop situated at the back of the lower hangar for the technicians to service and for the warhead to be fitted (these being stored separately) prior to use. Up on deck, all the 'ready use' ammunition for the anti aircraft weapons were stored in armoured lockers. As an added safety measure, the lockers containing the 'ready use' ordinance for the 105 mm guns (40 – 50 rounds per gun) benefited from water-cooling, cooling that in the heat of battle when fires were burning would hopefully prevent a 'home goal' being scored by the detonation of potentially hundreds of 105 mm rounds.

Protection at the waterline would be afforded from an armoured belt running the length of the ship. Contained within this armour would run the mains electricity ring, providing 4000 kW fed from four power plants, one on either side of the ship flanking an engine room, one in the bows and one aft. Each power plant had 'taps' for dividing up the ring, virtually

17   National Archive document ADMT 19137.

guaranteeing power for her guns, radar and lighting. To minimize the effect from battle damage and to ensure the continuation of operations, power supplies were often duplicated, for example the source of power for her 200 watt overhead lights on the hangar deck, running in rows, five metres apart, alternated between two different power plants. Also equipment such as electric motors situated in the engine and boiler rooms could be powered from either of two power stations.

Relative safety from mines would be afforded the ship by its own retractable bow protection device that would have allowed her to sweep her own path, and later, with the added counterpoise bulges, a buffer to the armoured belt would be offered, further protecting the ship from torpedoes and other ordinance striking her side.

Technologically she was to be one of, if not *the* most advanced ships in the German fleet.

Afloat

FROM MOBILISATION TO RATIONALISATION

Barely three years after the signing of the Anglo – German naval agreement, plans were afoot for the further expansion of the Kriegsmarine, a committee being set up in September of 1938 to consider the options. Raeder had secured from Hitler the assurance that, 'for his political purposes he would not need the fleet before 1946'. Hitler even stated that, 'political developments were in the making which would give us ample time for unhurried, peaceful naval expansion' and that therefore, 'he preferred the more powerful fleet even if it took longer to build, and gave [Raeder] directions to plan on that basis.' In accordance with Hitler's wishes for a powerful surface fleet, the famous 'Z' plan for naval expansion, which was at this time being prepared, would declare Germany's intention that the carrier *Graf Zeppelin* would be joined not by one other carrier as originally planned, but three. *Graf Zeppelin* and her sister (the so-called *Peter Straßer*) whose keel was still months off being laid were to be joined by two much larger carriers. In the new year Hitler once more reiterated to Raeder that he had six years to build a fleet, and based on this the 'Z' Plan gained official approval on 27 January 1939.

Work quickly began on the super-battleships envisaged by the 'Z' plan, but with the Nazi occupation of Czechoslovakia less than two months later, Raeder became concerned that Hitler had misjudged the feelings and likely reaction of other European powers. He felt the occupation of Czechoslovakia risked war with Great Britain, the most dominant maritime power in the world, a power that the Kriegsmarine was most certainly not in a position to fight. Admiral Dönitz, head of U-boat command, also had his concerns. Dönitz was sure that construction of the 'Z' plan ships would compel Germany's adversaries to expand their fleets, who with their greater construction capabilities would most certainly leave them behind in any ensuing arms race. Despite these concerns, on 28 April 1939, Hitler renounced the Anglo – German naval agreement.

Four months later, Germany invaded Poland for the planned 'reoccupation' of territories taken from Germany to form the Polish Republic shortly after World War I. Predicting that Great Britain would enter into the hostilities, on 31 August (the day before the invasion began) Raeder issued instructions defining the navy's role in the event of any ensuing war with Great Britain. Laid down by Hitler, 'Directive Number One' declared that in the event of England and France commencing hostilities against Germany, 'The Navy will concentrate on commerce destruction directed especially against England.'[18]

In the weeks before the invasion of Poland, Hitler had been able to secure the Eastern Front by means of the 'Nazi – Soviet pact', which divided up Poland between Russia and Germany along the lines of San-Vistula-Narew-Pisia, but no such pact had been agreed with the western powers. Thus, by the time the elderly armoured cruiser *Schleswig-Holstein* fired the opening rounds of the 'reoccupation' into the garrison on the Westerplatte of the Polish city of Danzig, German U-boats and warships were already stationed in the Atlantic in anticipation of coming events. Days later, as Hitler's naval staff had warned, Great Britain declared war on Germany, starting a conflict that eventually escalated into the Second World War.

When hostilities commenced on 3 September the *Graf Zeppelin* was 85 per cent complete. With the new developments in world affairs Grand Admiral Raeder issued the following orders on naval construction: 'The pre-war building programme is hereby cancelled. The new building programme will embrace, with equal priority:

1. The building of U-boats of the types recommended by U-boat command.
2. Continuation of the work on the five large ships - the battleships Bismarck and Tirpitz, the cruisers, Prinz Eugen and Seydlitz, and the aircraft carrier Zeppelin.
3. The building of additional destroyers, torpedo boats, minesweepers and trawlers as are required for the protection of coastal waters; the building of a number of S-boats.'[19]

Their level of completion saved these larger ships, but those ships that were in the earlier stages of construction would have to be scrapped. The 70,000-ton super-battleships would fall victim to Raeder's axe as would *Zeppelin's* sister ship the so-called *Peter Straßer*, her keel having been completed up to the armoured deck was broken up where it lay as both the steel and slipway were needed for the construction of U-boats and other more pressing war needs. The keels for the other two larger carriers would never be laid.

Hitler's belief that Germany was a continental power, his lack of understanding of naval affairs and the necessity of sea power, coupled with Raeder's lack of political ambition, would ensure that for much of the war the navy

18 Extract from: *Der Seekrieg* by Friedrich Ruge.

19 Extract from: *Memoirs* by Karl Dönitz

June 1940, Graf Zeppelin at the fitting-out yard. The two giant compressed air cylinders on her flight deck would be fitted in compartments between the catapult tracks, supplying compressed air to this apparatus. Bundesarchiv RM 25 Bild-62

had a chronic lack of steel, the lion's share of Germany's increasing output inevitably going to the army and the influential Herman Göring's Luftwaffe.

The entrance of Great Britain and her allies into the war was disastrous for the Kriegsmarine; having entered into a major construction programme on Hitler's assurance that there would be no war with Britain for at least six years, Germany's slipways were cluttered with the keels of ships that were doomed to never float. Not only were these great keels blocking the much-needed slipways, but months had been lost in the construction of U-boats and other more appropriate surface vessels for waging war against Great Britain. In such a short period of time Germany could not have hoped to build a fleet that could be a match for the Royal Navy. The ships of the Kriegsmarine, though powerful, would just not be numerous enough; the fleet that Germany had endeavoured to build would have been symbolic of Hitler's ego and the power he desired. Raeder had advised Hitler that if war was likely with the major sea powers in the not too distant future, then U-boats were needed. U-boats could have caused havoc amongst Britain's convoys bringing in materials for the continuation of the war, using stealth over displays of surface power. Raeder commented that, 'building a fleet for political purposes demonstrated Hitler's naval thinking. He was concerned with warships – particularly battleships – purely as symbols of power and he showed little interest in their deployment and use in actual operations.'[20]

With the construction of the proposed fleet barely started and with the existing ships still suffering teething problems (some of them had just started major overhauls) it would appear that Hitler got more than he bargained for when his forces crossed into Poland. The fleet just was not ready. The *Graf Zeppelin* was afloat but far from complete, still lacking much essential equipment.

Great Britain and her allies however had no way of knowing the state of readiness of the German carrier and thought that she was much nearer completion than she actually was. Their Lordships of Britain's Royal Navy greeted news of the imminent completion of the *Graf Zeppelin* and the battleship *Bismarck* with trepidation. The problem they faced was that even though the Royal Navy was indeed powerful, it largely consisted of ageing ships. Only the Royal Navy's as yet to be completed *King George V* class of battleship could be a match for the speed and power of the *Bismarck*, but the German carrier could cause more of a problem. Of a similar scale to Great Britain's more modern carriers but coupled with the incredible seaworthiness of Germany's ships, she was built to the Tirpitz principal that 'above all a ship must stay afloat'. She was originally intended to carry 50 – 60 aircraft, including Bf 109T fighters (the suffix 'T' standing for the German word for carrier, 'Träger'), Stuka dive-bombers and a Fieseler torpedo attack aircraft, but even when this number was revised downwards to a combined total of 43, coupled with her powerful anti-aircraft weaponry, and the most powerful surface-to-surface weaponry on any carrier then afloat, a task force of *Bismarck, Gneisenau, Prinz Eugen* and the *Graf Zeppelin* would have been a frightening proposition. A German publisher printed a fleet wall chart giving a false silhouette of the as yet incomplete *Graf Zeppelin* shortly after the start of war. The Allies used these misleading drawings, meaning that not only were they unsure how to fight it, but also, what it looked like.

The imbalance in carrier forces was adjusted somewhat in Germany's favour just weeks into the war, when HMS *Courageous* was torpedoed by U-29 (Kptlt. Otto Schuhart) while on an anti-submarine patrol; sinking in just 15 minutes she took her Captain and 518 men with her. Except for faulty torpedoes HMS *Ark Royal* would have been sunk just days before the *Courageous* when U-39 fired three torpedoes at the *Ark* only to have all three explode prematurely (a fault that would save many British ships, from battleships to cargo ships, in the first years of the war). Had *Graf Zeppelin* been completed in time for these early days of the war, when the Allies' carrier force essentially consisted of aging British vessels, and when German carrier aircraft would have had the upper hand over those of Great Britain,

---

20 Extract from: *Grand Admiral* by Erich Raeder

there would be little that could touch her. *Graf Zeppelin* could have reigned supreme, her battle group decimating Britain's convoys.

However, contrary to what was believed in Britain, *Graf Zeppelin* was not near completion. She had been spared the breakers yard but now she languished in Kiel harbour, a survivor of Raeder's war measures and what Dönitz called 'the most tragic situation in naval history,' going on to add, 'On the outbreak of war the Commander-in-Chief immediately gave orders that all work on capital ships not yet actually launched should cease forthwith, that the building programme envisaged in the Z-plan should be suspended and that the construction of the types of U-boats proposed by me [Dönitz] in my memorandum on the U-boat command war game 1938 – 39 should be taken in hand at once and as a matter of extreme urgency'.[21] So urgent was this need for more U-boats that U-boat Command would look to source additional boats from Estonia.

In these early days of the war, before the fall of France and the occupation of her Atlantic ports and all their repair facilities, there was little urgency placed on completing the *Graf Zeppelin*. Raeder felt that a carrier was too vulnerable and not useful enough in the North Sea where land based aircraft could operate. Lacking any peacetime experience of operating this type of vessel he did not fully appreciate the potency of a carrier prowling the Atlantic, and only later would he seriously consider the possibility of sending her out in the company of cruisers to this ocean. Though in all fairness, with the fall of France and the seizure of her Atlantic port at this point in the war unimaginable, any Atlantic operations were risky propositions that involved running the gauntlet of passing Great Britain and her forces on both the outward and homeward-bound legs of each and every mission.

Being an oil burner, *Graf Zeppelin* lacked the range of the diesel powered pocket battleships and would have been dependent on frequent rendezvous with supply ships. When it came to the inevitable journey home, any damage incurred on the mission that either slowed her down or hindered her fighting capability could be fatal. So for now, incomplete and without aircraft, the *Graf Zeppelin*'s power rested purely in the fact that she was. Her existence alone enough to cause panic in Great Britain, and, as with the existence of the *Tirpitz*, would tie up units of the Royal Navy in anticipation of her breakout.

---

21   Extract from: *Memoirs* by Karl Dönitz

Where the Sky Meets the Sea

CONTROL OF THE AIR

The foundations of navy flying in Germany were laid surprisingly quickly after the end of the Great War. As early as 1924 two men had been assigned to look after the navy's interests in the aviation world; these were Captain Lohmann, head of naval transportation (who was also involved in other secret developments such as illegal U-boats in the Netherlands) and Captain Lahs, who by posing as a private buyer would purchase seaplanes destined for use with the navy. In the mid-1920s ten planes were ordered from Heinkel, allegedly destined for South America; in reality they were shipped to Sweden for assembly from where they were flown to Germany, disassembled and packed away for later use.

Navy officers were given 'private' flying lessons from 1927, and a naval air arm came into being proper in 1928 thanks to Captain Zander. Zander had succeeded in establishing this air arm by arguing that aircraft, hitherto illegal under the Treaty of Versailles, were needed for gunnery targets, rather than the need for the aircraft themselves. It was also he who saw to the creation of 'Air Services Incorporated', a private company from which the navy would 'rent' aircraft to tow targets for their gunners to shoot at.

In August of the same year that Air Services Incorporated came into being, the liner *Bremen* was launched. She would carry a 'catapult aeroplane, this device enabling the mail to reach Bremerhaven or New York many hours earlier than if they had been transhipped in the usual way. Three days have been saved on delivery of mails between New York and Berlin. The catapult plant itself is erected on a wheel rim and rotates on a pin so that it can be swung round to either side of the ship. Planes of up to a total weight of 3.5 tons can be started from the catapult. The aircraft used on the *Bremen* can maintain an average speed of 118 mph and can carry approximately 440 lb of mail.'[22] *Bremen*'s keel was laid in June 1927 and an increased knowledge of streamlining, made her designers decide to

---

22 *Shipping Wonders of the World*, part 6, p. 187

give her a bulb-shaped stem below the waterline, in place of the hitherto universally used fine stem. This innovation gave the ship buoyancy forward and also prevented her from plunging in rough seas and lifting her propellers.'[23] This same 'bulb-shaped stem' would appear on the future ships of the Kriegsmarine, *Graf Zeppelin* included. The catapult was yet another civilian application for what would ultimately become a military appliance, the 'mail delivery pilots' perhaps the navy flyers of the future.

In 1933, three years before the *Graf Zeppelin*'s keel had even been laid, Herman Göring's appointment as head of the newly formed Ministry for Air (pertaining to be a Civil authority, it was in reality a guise from which the Luftwaffe was formed) would start a series of events that could only be detrimental to the carrier's future. Göring had strong feelings about navy flying and was prepared to fight for control of the navy's aircraft. He argued that the navy and army did not need their own air forces, a third force, the newly created Luftwaffe, being better suited to fulfil this role. Party leader Herman Göring, who like Raeder was a veteran of the Great War fifteen years before, would of course head the Luftwaffe, but neither man would ever see eye to eye. Raeder, the upright military man, servant of the nation, devoid of political ambition (Raeder was never a member of the Nazi party) and Göring, the power hungry National Socialist, would clash on many occasions, Raeder commenting that 'He [Göring] possessed a colossal vanity' and that they were complete opposites both personally and ideologically.[24] Raeder believed in and fought hard for a separate naval air arm, not out of any personal desire to expand the scope of his influence or power, but because he thought this was best for Germany. Göring would claim that naval units were actually part of the air force, the navy countering this by declaring that aircraft were 'not an auxiliary naval weapon, but part of the fleet to the same extent as torpedo boats, submarines etc.'[25] Göring countered Raeder's aerial ambitions with the repeated assertion that 'everything that flies belongs to us!' (meaning the air force), and his persuasive powers over Hitler would ultimately ensure that Raeder failed. The wrangling however would drag on for years to come, no definitive agreement being reached until 1939 despite many attempts to resolve the differences of the two forces.

In December 1936, as the *Zeppelin*'s keel was being laid, amid the battle of wills between Göring and Raeder the Luftwaffe offered the navy: one carrier fighter squadron, three carrier multi-purpose and one carrier Stuka squadron up to 1 October 1938, increasing to six multi-purpose and two fighter squadrons by 1942. This diminished the offensive capability desired by the navy who had requested two more fighter carrier squadrons and another Stuka squadron (presumably wanting enough aircraft to equip both planned carriers).

The navy originally had designs on a variety of new aircraft to fulfil the

---

23 *Shipping Wonders of the World*, part 6, p. 184

24 Extract from: *Grand Admiral* by Erich Raeder

25 Extract from: *The Luftwaffe and the War at Sea 1939 – 1945* by David Isby

various roles required of a carrier-borne air force, several Arado aircraft and a Fieseler being in the running. However, each aircraft offered was of the now outdated biplane design and with the exception of the Fieseler all would be unsuccessful in their bid to become carrier aircraft. Fieseler's successful biplane design, the Fi 167,

The Fi 167, Graf Zeppelin's purpose built torpedo bomber. Bundesarchiv Bild 146-1977-110-06

was accepted for use on board, and space for a total of 20 of these aircraft was reserved on each carrier. The Fi 167s were to be the most numerous aircraft carried, operating in the roles of reconnaissance aircraft/torpedo bombers and smoke layers. For the carrier's fighter contingent, a late offer of Messerschmitt Bf 109 aircraft would be accepted. An infinitely more desirable fighter than any of the outdated biplane designs the navy had looked at, the Bf 109s were of a much more modern design and almost 45 mph faster than the already obsolete attempt offered by Arado (as the Bf 109 developed this advantage would increase to nearly 110 mph).

Messerschmitt would base its initial batch of ten aircraft destined for

Aerial shot of a Bf 109 and a Ju 87 aircraft. Along with the purpose built Fieseler, variants of each of these aircraft converted for carrier use were to be carried. Bundesarchiv Bild 101i-429-0646-31

the carrier on a conversion proposal put forward early in 1939. This proposal saw Bf 109E-1 aircraft already on the production line receiving modified wings that would be slightly increased in span; the increase offered greater lift that would aid take-off from a short runway and give a slower landing speed, helpful on a carrier's deck. Other modifications would include the addition of catapult points, an arrestor hook for catching the brake wire on the carrier's flight deck, and strengthening of the airframe to help it withstand the forces exerted upon it during catapulting. Designated the Bf 109T-0 these first ten aircraft were to be immediately supplemented by another sixty purpose-built aircraft designated

Forward view of Ju 87C with wings in folded position.

Bf 109T-1s. In all, ten of these aircraft were to be carried at any one time. There was also to be a specially built variant of the Stuka dive-bomber, the Ju 87C, with provision onboard for 13 of them. Like the Fieseler, the Ju 87C would be equipped with folding wings[26], an innovation that greatly aided the storage of aircraft on the hangar decks. As both of these aircraft were of the fixed undercarriage type (meaning their landing gear was not retractable) – a hindrance to successful emergency landings on the water – it was considered necessary to equip them with jettison-able undercarriages. Unlike the Fieseler the Ju 87C was considered to be a potential catapult aircraft, and as such would be equipped with catapult points and an arrestor hook like those attached to the Bf 109. It was the intention that later versions of this aircraft should benefit from an automated system for

Side view of Ju 87C with wings in folded position.

---

26   Unlike the Fieseler and the Ju 87, the wing structure of the Bf 109 would not be altered to allow its wings to fold.

folding its wings.

In August of 1938 the foundations were laid for the *Graf Zeppelin's* first 'Carrier Group' (Trägergruppe). Based at Kiel-Holtenau, one of the two proposed carrier bases (the other being Bremerhaven), Trägergruppe 186 was initially to consist of a squadron each of Bf 109Bs and Ju 87As, with an additional squadron of Bf 109s promised for the following year. These aircraft would of course only be a stopgap, merely a training aid for the aircrews while they waited for the specially built shipboard variants of these machines to be completed.

Carrier Group established, clarification as to under whose authority these and other shore-based navy fliers would operate and what roles the air force and naval air arm would play still did not come, the arguing continuing with Göring as reluctant as ever to release aircraft to the navy. The navy would insist it needed from the air force 62 air squadrons dedicated to naval purposes (an increase of 37 squadrons on what they originally declared they needed). Göring would claim that 13 air force squadrons would be far better than the reconnaissance and combat squadrons of the proposed naval air units.[27] Finally, on the same date as the 'Z' plan got official approval, 27 January 1939, Göring and Raeder finally came to an agreement as to aircraft and their role in naval flying. Defining operational areas, size of units to be provided and command organisation, it was agreed that the navy would get nine long-distance reconnaissance squadrons, 18 multipurpose squadrons, two shipboard squadrons and 12 carrier squadrons up to 1941. Negotiations on the subject were declared ended, the agreed protocol signed on 3 February. The agreement supposedly gave tactical command of all air units assigned to the navy to the Commander-in-Chief, Navy. In reality, Raeder had had to succumb to Göring. The navy had gained little, still dependant on the air force for the allocation of aircraft, even requiring signatures from Commander-in-Chief, Air, before training of naval air personnel could take place. Ultimately, Göring would bypass even this agreement by cutting allocations of aircraft for the navy, while at the same time creating his own Flieger Corps X (Air Corps X), dedicated to operations over the sea.

Raeder had tried his best to form the naval air wing, even asking Hitler to clarify the situation, but was disappointed with Hitler's reply and commented that, 'Göring had had his way, for the agreement laid down that the air force too would wage war at sea. Aircraft would be detailed for duty with the navy only when required for reconnaissance purposes or to take part in tactical air battle in the event of fleet engagements. Types and numbers of aircraft to be constructed for these naval air formations, their organisation and training would all remain to be decided by the air force.'[28] Göring would not even give consideration to navy requests as to the type of

27   Extract from: *Grand Admiral* by Erich Raeder

28   Extract from: *Memoirs* by Karl Dönitz

planes to be assigned to these marine matters. Instead of the modern long-range reconnaissance aircraft the navy needed he provided them with the already obsolete He 115 and the He 111J, an aircraft that was not sufficient to carry out the duties required of it. Obstinate as ever, Göring would also see to it that co-operation between air force and navy would be further hampered. 'Moreover the Luftwaffe used its own procedure as regards navigational grid squares, cipher keys, and radio wave-lengths, which further complicated cooperation with the Navy.'[29] Göring, toying with the navy, had no intention of co-operating for the good of the nation. The arrogance demonstrated by Göring's Luftwaffe continued even once combat had begun. Advised by the navy that aerial torpedoes were far more likely to sink ships, their aircraft persisted in bombing them, it being November of 1940 before the Luftwaffe carried out its first successful aerial torpedo attack as torpedoes were considered to be 'uneconomical'.

With the Luftwaffe responsible for aircraft production, research into maritime aircraft was greatly curtailed without the navy ever having being informed, as was the development of aerial torpedoes which the navy had had operational since 1932. The lack of a decent maritime aircraft would greatly hinder U-boat and surface vessel operations throughout the war, the halt in torpedo development leaving Germany's aerial torpedoes less effective than they otherwise might have been; though torpedoes were still the most effective way of delivering an aerial assault against shipping, further development had been needed as they were often not powerful enough to sink a merchant ship never mind an armoured warship of the Royal Navy.

Göring's complete disregard for the agreed protocol of early 1939 that was supposed to define the aeroplane's role in navy flying and the navy's operational areas, ultimately resulted in Hitler intervening, a disaster for the naval air command; Hitler dictated his own protocol that declared that all naval air units were to operate under the control of Commander-in-Chief, Air. Inevitably, the Luftwaffe went on to strip its maritime sister of its assets, until the last Air Group was transferred back to the command of the air force towards the end of 1941. This process started a month after the war began, though it did come with the promise of more carrier squadrons by way of compensation.

The ill feeling between the two organisations would be reflected in the alliance that would have existed on board the carrier between air force and navy staff. Purely professional, it would not be one that would come naturally. It being observed in 1941 that, 'quarters are already being built and it has been necessary to start low down because the ship carries a large number of Air Force personnel who have to have quarters of their own, completely separate from those of the Naval personnel'.[30] Air force and navy personnel would lead separate existences; deck 'D' for example

---

29   Extract from: *Der Seekrieg* by Friedrich Ruge

30   National Archive document: ADMT 19137

was divided down the middle, port for the navy, and, separated by the upper hangar deck, the air force would occupy starboard. Above these, the officers who were in residence on deck 'A' would clump together[31], navy and air force separated by the hospital and quarters for the medical staff. Even the Officers' Mess on deck 'A' was divisible into two parts, navy and air force. Onboard duties being similarly divided, 'the work onboard is arranged on the principal that fixed fittings are to be assigned to the Navy, and movable ones to the Air Force; the maintenance of the arrestor wire system is the concern of the Navy, the operation of the arrestor system is the concern of the Air Force; the working of the lifts comes under the Navy; the maintenance of the catapults and the working of the compressors under the Navy, catapulting under the Air Force.'[32] Of course the navy would occupy the majority of space onboard the *Graf Zeppelin*, her crew list of 1941 consisting of:

> **108 Officers (51 Air Force)**
> **121 Warrant officers (53 Air Force)**
> **318 Petty officers – Sergeants (58 Air Force)**
> **1089 Crew (155 Air Force)**
> **25 Petty officers specialised in flying matters**
> **30 Cadets**
> **2 Barbers**
> **5 Tailors**
> **4 Cobblers**
> **18 Cooks and waiters**
> **Totalling 1720 persons.**

In the first months of the war the lack of air cover being provided from the still incomplete carrier's deck was not that big a problem to the Kriegsmarine. Within weeks of the war starting, British air cover far out to sea became virtually nonexistent after *U-29* (Lt Schuhardt) torpedoed and sunk the carrier HMS *Courageous*, sister ship to HMS *Furious* (*Furious* had been inspected by the 'K' office back in 1935 for those initial guiding pictures of what the *Graf Zeppelin* would be), whilst employed on anti-submarine duties. Following the loss of *Courageous*, the Royal Navy decided that carriers were too big a risk for anti-submarine duties and withdrew them from the Atlantic leaving the U-boats to their prey.

As Germany had no pre-war experience with carriers operating in fleet formation, it is unlikely that Raeder fully grasped what a useful tool he would have had in such a vessel operating far offshore, with its own aircraft attacking or guiding in the U-boat wolf packs and armed raiders onto the British lifelines crossing every ocean. The *Graf Zeppelin* would have been a

---

31 At nearly 6 metres tall, each hangar deck had two decks running along their outsides, one above the other.

32 National Archive document: ADMT 19137

formidable weapon in the first months of the war when Great Britain was still trying to implement the convoy system; pickings would have been truly rich. However, during this time, 'Germany was waging war at sea without an air arm; that was one of the salient features of naval operations, a feature that was as much out of line with contemporary conditions as it was decisive in its effect' (Karl Dönitz). In these early days of the war, 'For its own reconnaissance and tactical requirements the navy was to be provided only with the following naval air units:

> **9 squadrons of flying boats for long-range reconnaissance**
> **18 multi-purpose squadrons for reconnaissance and anti-submarine operations, etc.**
> **12 carrier-borne squadrons**
> **2 ship-borne squadrons of catapult aircraft.'[33]**

These meagre naval air units represented nowhere near the number of aircraft that Raeder and the O.K.M. felt they needed, but Göring had the clout with Hitler, and he had the aircraft. The navy would take what they were given. By May 1940, Raeder himself was suggesting a hold be put on any further work on the *Graf Zeppelin*. Her anti-aircraft weaponry had already been assigned to other more pressing needs; to regain possession of this weaponry could only be done at the expense of the army, and, besides, the delay in the fire control for her heavy artillery meant that though completed it was not yet fitted. With the war starting to get into full swing it was looking like the earliest possible date for completion of *Graf Zeppelin* would be January 1941, however her heavy artillery would not be fully installed for at least a year after that, and even then she would still be in need of 12 months of sea trials; this delay was no doubt caused by the original fire control system for these weapons having been delivered to Russia as part of the 'Treaty of Frontier Regulation and Friendship' of 1939 that divided Poland between the two nations.

It would take great expenditure in resources and manpower needed elsewhere to complete the vessel, in a war in which Germany was winning victory after victory and that many believed was as good as over. Probably originating from the 'K' office, a report taken from Raeder's personal notes dated 29 April 1940 concludes: 'It is not expected that the carrier will be ready for duty during this war, however the necessary personnel and weaponry, needed for the completion of the carrier, could be usefully used for urgent tasks for the war effort.' The Grand Admiral having made his mind up, with only a finite number of shipyard workers, and the navy receiving a mere five per cent of the country's total steel production, had to rationalise. Following the recommendations of the 'K' office, Raeder ordered a moratorium to be placed on any further work. The 150 mm artillery pieces destined for the *Graf Zeppelin*, some of which, if not all, had already been at least partially installed on-board were dismantled for shipping to the newly conquered Norway, where they were installed as coastal defence batteries.

---

33 Extract from: *Der Seekrieg* by Friedrich Ruge,

Completion had taken a step backwards.

Installation of one of the Graf Zeppelin's 150 mm gun emplacements. It would not be long before they were dismantled for shipping to Norway. Bundesarchiv RM 25 Bild-49

Rear shot of a 150 mm gun emplacement. Directed from one of two 'fire control' rooms (one for each side of the ship), data could be sent to the battery on the other side of the ship via an exchange, allowing each battery to be used through it's own transmitting room from the other side. Bundesarchiv RM 25 Bild-50

As a direct result of the suspension of work on the carrier, construction of the sixty Bf 109T-1s (being built under contract by Fieseler) then being assembled for her also stopped, these aircraft being completed later in the year without their planned carrier aircraft components as the re-designated Bf 109T-2s; by the following June they would be dispatched with JG77 to Norway.[34] Like the Bf 109s, the Ju 87Cs then under construction were similarly completed minus their carrier additions[35] for use elsewhere, only the initial batch of 12 Fieselers were completed in their intended configurations, this being done shortly after hostilities began.

---

34 The increased wing span of these aircraft that were originally intended for carrier operations gave them a slight advantage over more conventional Bf 109s when taking off and landing from the temporary and often short runways of Norway.

35 Though they did retain the jettison-able under-carriage.

The War Years

THE RACE FOR COMPLETION

With the commencement at the end of February 1940 of the breaking of what existed of the *Peter Straßer*, followed two months later by Raeder's decision to postpone completion of the *Graf Zeppelin*, Germany's carrier programme had effectively been shelved. On 6 July 1940 the *Graf Zeppelin* would undertake her first voyage, not into active service as was the major concern across the water in Great Britain, but into hiding owing to concerns about damage from air raids. Concerns that were well founded, the Royal Air Force (R.A.F.) at the request of the Royal Navy had already evaluated the possibility of striking her while she was still completing rather than face her on the high seas.

With her engine room machinery not yet fully operational, *Graf Zeppelin* had to be taken under tow from Kiel to Gotenhafen (now Gdynia). By the time of her departure from Kiel she was 5.2 metres longer than when launched 19 months before, her overall length having increased earlier in the year as she was fitted with the new 'Atlantic bow'.

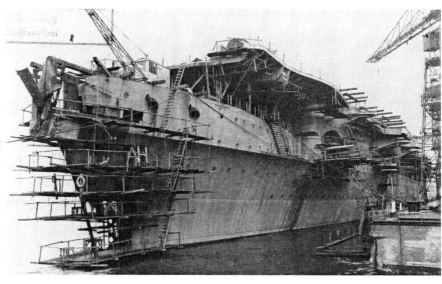

Construction of the Atlantic bow. During this retro-fit one of the port side anchors was permanently removed and it's hawse covered over. Bundesarchiv RM 25 Bild-57

The flared, sweeping Atlantic bow, replacing the more traditional almost vertical one, would improve her seaworthiness and came as a result of lessons learned in the aftermath of the *Gneisenau* and *Scharnhorst* action with the British armed merchant cruiser S.S. *Rawalpindi* late in 1939. Mountainous Atlantic seas had flooded the forward turrets of the two battleships doing more damage to the sisters than the shell hits from *Rawalpindi*'s six-inch guns. The Atlantic bow was a must if the *Graf Zeppelin* was ever to see the action Grand Admiral Raeder one day hoped she would. For it was clear to all that the Atlantic was where she would ply her trade. The North Sea, dangerously boxed in and easily within striking distance of the land-based aircraft of the Royal Air Force, was no place for a carrier to operate, and would have been completely unnecessary, the Luftwaffe's own land-based aircraft being perfectly capable of operating there.

1940 would see the Kriegsmarine, much to everyone's surprise, gaining easier access to the Atlantic thanks to the fall of France. Throughout May and June of 1940, U-boat Command in anticipation of France's impending defeat, had had a train waiting, loaded with all that would be needed in men and equipment to maintain their U-boats in newly acquired French harbours along the Atlantic coast. The day after France's surrender, the train and its cargo departed for the Biscay ports.

Germany's rapid success against France had stunned everyone, including Germany, who, with the opening up of these Atlantic ports to their own shipping, was now even stronger, the benefits to Hitler's war machine being many. For the smaller craft such as submarines their radius of action was significantly increased, as days were cut off the time spent travelling to and from the area of operations, giving them longer on station in their patrol area, effectively increasing the number of U-boats in service (the days these craft had spent travelling to and from their area of patrol were effectively lost days, the boat not being in action). In fact the number of boats on active service did increase, as now even the smaller coastal submarines were suddenly found able to operate out in the Atlantic from these captured French ports against convoys heading to and from Great Britain. Access to these ports and their facilities also helped free up space in boatyards back in Germany, relieving them of some of their maintenance workload for U-boats, and allowing them to concentrate on building new submarines. The acquisition of the giant dry dock at St Nazaire, built for the liner *Normandie* and measuring three hundred and fifty metres long by fifty metres wide, meant that even the largest of the surface ships of the Kriegsmarine could be dry docked when needed. No longer having to run the gauntlet of passing Great Britain at the start and finish of every mission, a journey in which any damage to a ship of the Kriegsmarine that even slightly affected the ship's fighting performance or speed could have meant destruction. Now, once out into the Atlantic, there would be no need to complete the perilous journey home, safety being available all along France's western coast. Here the ships could re-arm, re-fuel and repair.

With the success throughout that first summer of the war of Germany's pocket battleships and the famous armed merchant cruisers (heavily armed raiders disguised as merchant ships), expectations and confidence in the surface fleet had run high, but by the time *Bismarck* was commissioned in August of 1940 the lack of an operational carrier was making itself felt. Raeder would later comment, '[*Bismarck*]... suffered one great disadvantage, which the enemy did not share; she would have no accompanying, integrated air forces to protect her. On the other hand the enemy with his numerous aircraft carriers and airfields could project his air strikes against us where ever our ships might be. This was recognizably a terrific handicap; yet, with no aircraft carriers of our own, there was nothing we could do about it....'[36] *Bismarck*'s historic six-day sortie of May the following year ended with the duel to the death that the British had long planned and that many in Germany realised was inevitable. Long before *Bismarck*'s fateful last sortie, Captain Karl Topp, Commander of the *Tirpitz*, during many 'war games' was unable to come up with an outcome other than the destruction of *Bismarck*. However, at Admiralty House in London, 16 months before that fateful mission, many sleepless nights were had worrying about *Bismarck*, then believed to be nearing completion. Much of the concern centred on the apparent level of completeness of the mighty *Bismarck* in comparison to the Royal Navy's own modern, but still completing battleship *King George V* (K.G.V.), and the others of her class. A request by Winston Churchill to consider launching *K.G.V.* with a dummy turret in place of the lagging real two-gun turret, which was causing the delay, is indicative of the level of concern.

However, truth be known, back in January of 1940, it was not *Bismarck* that worried their Lordships the most, but another ship, also believed to be nearing completion, one of a new generation, with the ability to reconnoitre vast distances, seek out and destroy both convoy and warship alike, while herself remaining safely out of range of even the biggest guns. The extract below, taken from a secret British document dated 29 January 1940 clearly demonstrates the level of concern: 'it is the aircraft carrier *GRAF ZEPPELIN* which is likely to provide our most disagreeable problem. If this ship, accompanied by *BISMARCK* or one of the *SCHARNHORSTS*, were to break out, we should have to be prepared for very serious depredations on our trade. In good weather the aircraft carrier could reconnoitre some 20,000 square miles in one day and could hardly fail to locate some of our large convoys. Her reconnaissance would serve equally to defend the attackers from our hunting groups. This power of evasion might enable raids to be pressed into the

---

36 Extract from: *Grand Admiral* by Erich Raeder

western approaches, our most vulnerable area.

The conclusion is that the *BISMARCK* herself is not likely to prove the menace that would at first seem likely. It is the aircraft carrier which is going to turn the scales in favour of any raider.'[37] For though statistically *Graf Zeppelin* might have been vaguely similar to Great Britain's modern carriers,[38] *Ark Royal* or *Illustrious*, her aircraft certainly were not. The Bf 109 fighter aircraft, Stuka dive-bombers and Fieseler torpedo aircraft intended for operations from the German carrier were fearsome opponents for Britain's obsolete carrier aircraft, that largely consisted of Sea Gladiators (carrier-borne biplanes operating as fighters), the Fairy Swordfish reconnaissance/torpedo bombers and the Blackburn Skua fighter/dive bombers, none of which were a match for the fast, heavily armed Bf 109Ts. Against this lacklustre opposition,[39] the Bf 109s 20 mm canons would have made short work of any formations of these aircraft unfortunate enough to be intercepted, smashing an airborne attack long before it came within the range from which aerial torpedoes could be released, *Zeppelin's* anti-aircraft armament acting as final goal-keeper for any would-be attackers that slipped through the fighter screen.

Zeppelin's aircraft, operating in a variety of roles, could seek out and destroy British convoys, defend against attacking aircraft and, in a reconnaissance role, steer their own battle group away from confrontation with superior British forces.

The decision was made soon after the two ships' apparent level of completion were known (*Bismarck* and *Graf Zeppelin*) to try to deal with the giants inside their harbours before they were even operational. Destroying or at least badly damaging them from the air pre-commissioning, was infinitely preferable to hunting, finding and confronting on the high seas. By February of 1940 the Air Ministry had already received a request for at least the *Bismarck* to be bombed, with the then First Lord of the Admiralty, Winston Churchill, putting the idea forward in a letter dated 28 January 1940. Plans of attack against the *Graf Zeppelin* would soon follow. On 27 March a meeting was held at 'the Admiralty' in London and a document stamped MOST SECRET containing the minutes of that meeting produced. Beginning with a brief summary on each ship and then listing the possibilities for striking at both battleship and carrier in their respective harbours, that document is reproduced below.

---

37   National archive number ADM/10617

38   Though she was to carry significantly less aircraft.

39   It would be 1942 before the Fleet Air Arm was operating Sea Hurricanes and Seafires, actually Hurricanes and Spitfires adapted for carrier use.

Most Secret
Methods Of Attack On German Ships
Bismarck And Graf
Zeppelin

Minutes of meeting held at the Admiralty
on Wednesday, 27th March
Presided over by captain C.S. Daniel (D. of P.)

List of present…

Information

Graf Zeppelin

1. The latest information concerning the present position of the
    Graf Zeppelin indicated that she had probably commenced her
    trials but had possibly returned to Kiel for adjustments. Subject
    to this information being correct, it was considered that this
    ship would be finally complete during April or early May.

Bismarck

2. Is lying at the Steinwerder Ufer at Hamburg, being completed
    by Blohm and Vos Shipyard, and is not expected to be ready to
    commence trials before June at the earliest.

Possibilities Of Attack On Bismarck At Hamburg

3. (a) <u>Bombing</u>   This is precluded as long as our present bombing
    policy remains in force.
    (b) <u>Torpedo Attack</u>   In her present position the Bismarck
    does not present a torpedo target.
    (c) <u>Mines</u> It is hoped to commence laying M. [*magnetic*] mines in
    April off the mouth of the river Elbe in addition to other bases,
    but in order to avoid the possibility of a mine being dropped on
    shore or a mud bank, or the splash of a mine entering the water
    being seen, it was not considered desirable to lay mines farther
    up the river in the vicinity of Hamburg.

Attack Upon The Graf Zeppelin At Kiel

4. (a) <u>Bombing</u>   As long as this ship remains alongside, our pres-
    ent bombardment policy will preclude this being carried out.
    (b) <u>Torpedo Attack</u>   The R.A.F. torpedo bombers cannot
    reach this vicinity. Attack by carrier-borne aircraft would be
    possible if the ship were found to be occupying the berth that

she was last reported at.

(c) <u>Mining</u> It is anticipated that mines will be laid in Kiel Bay and the harbour approaches in April. Subsequently, depending on the results obtained, mines may be laid closer into the Kiel Fjiord [sic].

GENERAL CONCLUSIONS.

RECONNAISSANCE.

5.   It was agreed that continuous and up-to-date Reconnaissance was essential before any form of attack could be carried out, and Air Commodore Stevenson stated that it was hoped increased reconnaissance would be available at a very early date.

BOMBING.

6.   Any attempt to attack these vessels in the close proximity of their dockyards was precluded by our existing bombing policy. If, however they could be located and attacked at sea during their trials, the following scale of attack should be carried out:

BISMARCK

-To be attacked with 2,000-lb AP bombs.
A very large number of aircraft would have to be employed in order to have a reasonable chance of causing serious damage.

GRAF ZEPPELIN

-To be attacked at once on the maximum scale possible. As the 500-lb bomb would be effective against this ship, the chances of damaging her seriously would be good.

7.   Air Commodore Stevenson, however, pointed out that it was very improbable that we should be able to obtain reconnaissance of the exact area in which these ships were carrying out their trials, and that even if this were obtained it would be most improbable that these ships would remain in that area until a striking force of bomber arrived. In addition, the Air Ministry were not anxious to cross and re-cross the heavily defended Schleswig area of North-West Germany unless a very high priority was placed on the operation. If, however, these ships proceeded into the North Sea, the heaviest scale of air attack could be employed.

8.   Should the present bombardment policy be extended in the near future, [it] sic would then have to be considered in relation to the numerous other targets of importance that would become available.

Torpedo Attacks.

9.   Kiel Bay and to the eastward are out of range of existing R.A.F. torpedo bombers. An attack on the GRAF ZEPPELIN at Kiel could be carried out from carrier-borne aircraft provided:

(a)   the ship was suitably berthed;

(b)   risk of heavy casualties is accepted.

10.   The BISMARCK at Hamburg is within range of carrier-borne aircraft torpedo attack, but in her present position did not present a suitable target.

Mining.

11.   This form of attack appeared to offer the best possibility of early action. Mine laying from aircraft is expected to commence on April 19th, and it is the intention that mines shall be laid off the mouths of the Elbe, Ems, and Jarde Rivers, as well as off Kiel, Neustadt, Swinemunde and Warnemunde. After the initial lay of about 200 mines it is proposed to concentrate a heavier scale of attack on the Kiel area with subsequent mines.

Submarines

12.   The possibilities of attack by submarines in Kiel Bay was discussed, but the lack of a base in the Baltic would preclude continuous operations.

It is not clear where the information regarding the *Graf Zeppelin's* apparent operational readiness came from; the author has certainly found no evidence of her being ready to commence sea trials in early 1940, the 'adjustments' reported at this time in all probability being the construction of her 'Atlantic bow'. Reports of her imminent completion were misguided to say the least, perhaps just part of the misinformation spread by both sides to convince one another of the power that neither possessed at this point, mere rumours, proliferated by the Kriegsmarine for the benefit of British spies. Britain certainly used such techniques, for example when concerns were rife that *Bismarck* would be ready long before *K.G.V.* Winston Churchill had suggested that, 'In the right way and in the right time we should spread about by every means in our power likely to be effective, that K.G.V. and P. of W. have been accelerated. This will act as a deterrent.'[40]

What is noteworthy from the above report are the differences in scale of attack recommended for the two different ships; 2000 lb AP (Armour Piercing) bombs for the heavy armour of the *Bismarck*, 500 lb for the *Graf Zeppelin*. The use of these relatively light bombs for the attack on the carrier would have had the advantage of allowing the aircraft to carry a greater number of bombs, increasing the chances of scoring multiple hits

40   *P. of W.* meaning *Prince of Wales*, sister ship to *King George V*

on her, and is indicative of the relatively light armour of the *Graf Zeppelin* in comparison to that of the *Bismarck*. The differing levels of armour on these ships are indicative of their different roles, *Bismarck*, floating fortress, designed to both give and take mighty blows in a form of battle which, except for the incredible range now involved, had remained unchanged for centuries; *Graf Zeppelin* operating far over the horizon, hopefully never meeting her foe, her aircraft delivering the ordinance, her armour of secondary importance.

Bismarck never was attacked in harbour and went on to cost the British their battlecruiser HMS *Hood* and 1400 of her crew. The carrier, though eventually gaining the attention of Guy Gibson (later of Dam Buster fame), suffered no damage at his hands.

By mid 1940, the Kriegsmarine, still without 'eyes in the sky', would be dealt a blow that would ensure that their ships would never have a clear vision as to what was happening over the horizon or under the dark night sky. In a frenzy of rationalisation, Hitler issued the order that would ultimately see Germany fall behind in many fields she once led, with a moratorium being issued on all research and development, the axe falling on, amongst other things, radar.

While Germany's sole carrier sat idle in occupied Polish waters, Great Britain was utilising her carrier fleet to the full, extending the air war to distant shores. With France out of the war since mid-1940, and Italy entering the war alongside Germany the balance of Mediterranean Sea power had tipped in favour of the Axis powers. Britain's pre-war strategy for control of the waters of the Mediterranean had relied on the powerful French fleet, but this was controversially put out of action in July 1940 by Admiral Summerville's Force 'H'; Summerville decimated his recent ally in harbour at Mers-El-Kabir after his ultimatum of fresh alliance under the cause of the Free French, or internment in a foreign port so as to avoid utilisation of these units by the Kriegsmarine, was turned down. As even this extreme action could not redress the imbalance in the Mediterranean, only ensure it did not increase, daring deeds were needed. So it was on 11 November 1940 that control of the Mediterranean Sea would tip permanently into the hands of the Royal Navy, an air strike by carrier-borne aircraft on the Italian harbour at Taranto adding another page to the Royal Navy's glorious history. The Taranto strike, the first of its kind, preceding Japan's more famous Pearl Harbour attack by more than 12 months, seriously damaged three battleships (all had to be beached to prevent their total loss) and two heavy cruisers whilst riding at anchor inside Taranto harbour, and did some damage to the harbour facilities, all for the loss of only two aircraft. The Royal Navy at a stroke had regained the upper hand both in hardware and, perhaps more importantly, psychologically.

Six months after the Taranto strike, the power of the carrier was once again demonstrated when on 27 May 1941, *Bismarck*, in fulfilment of

Admiral Topp's war game predictions of the previous year, after a mere six days loose in the Atlantic and glowing red from the fires that burnt deep inside her, succumbed to her wounds and sank.[41] After an epic chase from Greenland to Biscay, with the safety of home waters looming, and with her pursuers low on fuel and facing having to turn back for home, a single torpedo, delivered by a Fairy Swordfish flown from the deck of HMS *Ark Royal*, jammed her rudders 12 degrees over to port, slowing her down and preventing her from navigating the necessary course to safety, allowing her pursuers to close for the kill.

Bismarck's demise had been aided by Hitler's directive of the previous year that stopped research into radar, and ensured her Seetakt radar apparatus would be inferior to the radar sets being installed on board Royal Navy ships since early that same year. Equipped with this new technology, the cruiser HMS *Suffolk* had been able to maintain contact with *Bismarck* out of range of her 380 mm guns, so as to direct a superior force of Royal Navy vessels to their rendezvous. Forewarned being forearmed, the Royal Navy already possessed knowledge of the capabilities of the *Bismarck's* Seetakt radar set as they had removed the aerial and associated equipment of the Seetakt for evaluation from the wreckage of the *Graf Spee*, shortly after her scuttling in the mouth of the River Plate.

Had *Bismarck* sailed in the company of the *Graf Zeppelin*, it would seem inconceivable that her end would have come so quickly. With carrier aircraft providing reconnaissance for Admiral Lütjens on board the *Bismarck*, he would have known with certainty what lay over the horizon, and armed with this knowledge, having just sunk the *Hood*, history could have recorded him closing on the malfunctioning *Prince of Wales* and easily finishing her.[42] Alternatively, Lütjens could have used the carrier aircraft to carry out an air-strike on the *Prince of Wales*, fulfilling her destiny to be the first battleship on the open sea lost to aircraft seven months before her actual demise to Japanese aircraft in the South China Sea. The result of either of these scenarios would have been that all the ships in Lütjens's Battle Group made it to the Biscay ports and would undoubtedly have gone on to have very successful careers. The repercussions of such a success could have been far reaching; Great Britain, standing alone in the struggle, her troops minus much of their equipment after having been evicted from Continental Europe 12 months before, but thus far her Empire still intact, may well have sued for peace. Indeed by February 1941 many in Germany believed Britain was ready to capitulate.

Unfortunately for the 2000 sailors who died with the *Bismarck* that day, they had sailed without air cover, the above scenario just another 'what if' to be viewed in retrospect by armchair Admirals and Generals of the twenty-

---

41 The argument still rages as to whether her sinking was as a result of damage sustained in combat or as a result of her heavily battered hulk being scuttled by her own crew.

42 Not yet fully commissioned, she still had civilian technicians on board, and in the action against *Bismarck* all but one of the guns of her main armament malfunctioned.

first century and beyond. *Bismarck*'s tale being the epic that it is, owes more to the loss occurring on her maiden voyage than to the laurels of battle.

By early 1941, Germany's naval air arm finally made some headway, when aircraft of Group 40 were placed under the command of Karl Dönitz, head of U-boat Command. Dönitz had been desperate for reconnaissance aircraft to give his U-boats eyes in the sky, to aid them in their hunt for the elusive convoys. However, the granting of these aircraft to U-boat Command was not indicative of a change of heart on the part of Reichsmarschall Göring; Hitler had given Group 40 to Dönitz without Göring's knowledge while he was away shooting. On his return Göring was furious, calling a meeting the following month with the U-boat Commander to try to convince him to return the air group to his command; Dönitz refused and in his own words they parted 'bad friends'.[43] Göring's fury was no doubt added to by the strain the Luftwaffe was then under, losing over 1700 aircraft by the end of The Battle of Britain in October 1940, losses they had not had a chance to recover. The toll of this massive effort meant that by early 1941 they were struggling even to maintain the scope of air attacks against Great Britain. With little time to recuperate, commitments followed for the Balkan campaign, quickly followed by the invasion of Russia for which 60 per cent of Luftwaffe frontline aircraft would be committed; the last thing Göring needed was aircraft removed from under his command. With the fate of the *Graf Zeppelin* very much linked to that of the Luftwaffe, Göring's problem was *Zeppelin*'s problem; if he was short of aircraft she certainly was not going to get any.

The destruction in the aftermath of *Bismarck*'s sinking of Kriegsmarine supply ships scattered throughout the Atlantic, would seem to many to spell the end of Atlantic sorties for the large units of Raeder's navy. Yes, they could still operate from the occupied Biscay ports, but with the ability to re-fuel at sea gone, their range in ocean terms was not great (for example, in her present configuration, had she been complete, the *Graf Zeppelin* was capable of 6500 miles at 19 knots), and limited to what fuel they could carry. Range not the only problem, *Bismarck*'s loss had highlighted what a mistake Hitler had made in his directive of mid-1940 cancelling the research into radar, leaving *Bismarck* to fight virtually blind against a foe whose own radar had not only improved over the previous year but had surpassed the capabilities of the Seetakt. The supremacy of British air power at sea had also been evident during those bleak days of May 1941.

To be fair, *Bismarck* had been sent out to face her foe much as the *Prince of Wales* and *Repulse* would be later in the year and, just like the two British ships, her lack of air cover had proved her undoing. It was obvious that no further Atlantic operations could take place as long as Germany was without an aircraft carrier. Later this same year, Dönitz would complain to Hitler that when 'the U-boat arm and indeed the whole navy was called upon to fight without Aerial reconnaissance, [it] was one of the

---

43   Extract from: *Memoirs* by Karl Dönitz

gravest handicaps under which we suffered'. He added the following year, 'Historians will depict the struggle at sea during the Second World War in different ways, according to their nationality. But, that the German navy, in this twentieth century, the century of aircraft, was called upon to fight without an air arm and without Aerial reconnaissance of its own is wholly incomprehensible.'[44]

Less than a month after the victory against *Bismarck*, the other half of Britain's 1940 maritime fears, *Graf Zeppelin*, undertook another journey, again under tow, this time west, away from the soon to be created Eastern Front. Moved to Stettin for safekeeping, she moored on 21 June, a day ahead of 'undertaking Barbarossa', the invasion of Russia planned since the previous December. Barbarossa was intended to remove the perceived land-based threat from Russia. A directive issued ten days before the start of the offensive demonstrated the Führer's thinking: 'upon completion of undertaking Barbarossa – the taking of Russia – no serious threat to Europe by land will remain… The main effort of the armaments industry can be diverted to the Navy and Air Force.'[45] But many, Raeder included, felt it would have been better to finish off the war already going on with Great Britain. Hitler, always the General never the Admiral, failed to grasp the importance of the war at sea. 'His decision has been made in favour of the land war against Russia not the sea war with England,' wrote Raeder in his memoirs. Indeed, Hitler viewed the seas that surrounded continental Europe more as a moat that would keep his enemies out, where as Raeder, the lifelong seafarer, understood that these great masses of water were Britain's highway to colonial might, key to her power, where the war could be won or lost. Raeder believed wholeheartedly that Germany should have been focusing on Britain's convoys, increasing the number of commerce raiding vessels as quickly as could be, since, Germany's raiders were becoming more active. Instead, Hitler, shaken after the loss of *Bismarck* in the cold grey wastes of the Atlantic to the west (in future, whenever a Capital Ship was at sea, he would worry incessantly until its safe return), issued the debilitating order that 'no unnecessary risk' should be taken with the surface fleet. Somehow it was expected that the navy would win great victories at sea while avoiding all confrontation! For though Hitler contained in his head huge amounts of technical details on the ships of the fleet, often surprising experts with his level of knowledge, orders such as that of 'no unnecessary risk' only served to demonstrate his lack of understanding of the operation and deployment of such ships.

The depressing news of *Bismarck*'s loss in the Atlantic must have been balanced by the lightning victories to the east, coming as welcome news to all in the Reich. Hitler, confident of victory, less than a month after the commencement of operation Barbarossa, on 14 July issued directive 32, 'which looked to substantial reductions in both army and navy'. A supple-

44 Extract from: *Memoirs* by Karl Dönitz

45 Extract from: *Hitler War Directives 1939 – 1945* edited by H.R. Trevor-Roper

ment to this directive issued the same day would ensure that the moratorium on the completion of the carrier remained, directive number 32a stating, 'The Navy will continue its submarine programme. Construction will be limited to what is directly connected with this programme. Expansion of the armaments programme over and above this is to be stopped.'

As the Soviet army collapsed in defeat after defeat, falling back across the vast Russian plains, the bomber threat to the *Graf Zeppelin* quickly passed, allowing for her return in November, again under tow, back to her eastern anchorage at Gotenhafen (Gdynia). Completion was still nowhere in sight but at least she was safe.

Meanwhile, Hitler, victim of his own propaganda, truly believing that he was the greatest General the world had ever known, not content with issuing debilitating orders to the navy, meddled increasingly in military affairs, insisting that his Generals report to him all their orders, 'so that I have time to intervene in this decision if I think fit, and that my counter-orders can reach the front line troops in time.'[46] He demanded that Moscow must be taken before the end of the year; his Generals insisted that their armies must be allowed to dig in for the winter. Hitler's will prevailed and Army Group Centre attacked on 4 December. The attack failed, the Group taking enormous casualties.

Barbarossa would grind to a halt in early 1943 inside the decimated city of Stalingrad. With what many consider to be the turning point in the war, the 6th Army under General Paulus,[47] encircled and having already lost over 200,000 men, was forced to capitulate, 94,000 men being taken prisoner. Far from being the lightning victory Hitler envisaged, the Russian offensive had sucked in both men and materials in vast amounts. Even when Germany was winning, losses of fighter aircraft on the Eastern Front outpaced production.

Raeder had of course been right; Hitler should have finished Britain when her back was against the wall before entering into conflict in the east, for just five months after the launching of Barbarossa, Britain, still reigning control of the seas, was joined by America, her long-time aid and now ally. Victory would now be based on industrial capability. American industry, unaffected by the war and out of range of Germany's bombers would not be surpassed. Neither would Soviet Russia, aided by British and American ships supplying, via the Arctic convoys, weapons and materials to Russia's seemingly endless plebiscite, who in turn would march off to death in their tens of millions: A huge sacrifice that ultimately led to victory.

---

46   Extract from: *Hitler War Directives 1939 – 1945* edited by H.R. Trevor-Roper

47   His Commission to Field Marshal just before the collapse at Stalingrad (a rank that had never before surrendered) indicated to Paulus, Hitler's intention that he should fight on until the last.

Without Wings

RISE OF A TASK FORCE

As 1941 came to a close, *Graf Zeppelin's* future looked no brighter for the coming year. The war in Russia was still raging on, America in response to Japan's December attack on Pearl Harbour joined the war on the side of Great Britain and her allies, declaring war not just on Japan but Germany as well. It now seemed more likely than ever that an invasion of mainland Europe would follow. Thus, on 14 December 1941, Hitler issued orders for the defence of the whole of the Atlantic coastline, building it into 'a new west wall'. Vast amounts of steel, concrete and human resources were poured into the fortification of Europe's coastline.

1941 had seen aeroplanes and U-boats working in tandem out in the Atlantic, but as the year came to a close their operational effectiveness had declined as U-boat operations had progressed too far out into the Atlantic for the land-based aircraft to follow, once again pushing Germany's lack of an operational carrier to the forefront. Now, not only was the lack of carrier preventing sorties into the Atlantic by the Capital ships of the fleet, it was also affecting the effectiveness of the U-boats, leaving them blind, relying on chance to find the elusive convoys.

Though it was generally accepted that the Kriegsmarine needed its lone carrier to be operational before the surface fleet could again operate, in accordance with the 'Hitler directive' work was at a standstill on the *Graf Zeppelin*. Meanwhile, and rather perversely, 800 hundred men were removed from their usual role of maintaining U-boats to labour on the smashed hull of the *Gneisenau* and the broken engine room machinery of her sister *Scharnhorst*. The Kriegsmarine High Command along with the Führer were blinded by the power that was on show for all to see in the form of their battleships, 'ships of the line' evolved into their most powerful form. They had been unable to see the folly of their ways in leaving the carrier only partially completed.

Raeder was beginning to understand that the battleships had had their day, but persisted in trying to send them out on Atlantic operations long after this proved futile, maybe over-estimating the impact that the presence of these ships had on the planning and strategy of the Royal Navy. Indeed battleships could still pack a mighty punch, decimate a convoy and sink an unwary foe, but only if they were out on the open sea. Yes, they helped to contain some of the larger ships of the Royal Navy, which stood by in anticipation of a breakout, but at great expense in materials and manpower to maintain them and their entourage of smaller craft. With the surface fleet immobilised by the lack of an aircraft carrier, the U-boat arm was now the only viable force for operations in the Atlantic; like the battleships, they too were capable of tying up a multitude of enemy warships and aircraft, but with the ability to inflict proportionally larger losses at a much more reasonable outlay in men and materials.

On 26 November 1941, the head of U-boat command Karl Dönitz, aware that operations in the Atlantic by heavy ships were no longer possible, but that long delays in refitting and repairing his U-boats were being caused by the withdrawal of dockyard labour for the repair of these battleships, sent a memorandum to Grand Admiral Raeder[48], writing: 'U-boat command believes that it should be possible to reduce the time spent in dockyards and thus very considerably increase the number of U-boats available at any given time for operations. It urges therefore, that the provision of adequate maintenance personnel, as the most effective way of attaining this object, should be regarded as a measure of the highest priority and importance.

In the light of the general industrial situation, the navy cannot expect any influx of labour from outside and must therefore make the best use it can of the resources it possesses.

To this end, therefore, dockyard personnel should be employed on the building or repair *only of such vessels as are indispensable to the prosecution of the war.*

In view of the urgent need of maintenance personnel for the U-boat arm, U-boat command is of the opinion that the whole question of the repair of battleships and cruisers and of building and repair of destroyers should be re-examined in the light of the principle enunciated above. In other words, are these types of vessels essential for the prosecution of the war?

We are in conflict with the two strongest maritime powers in the world, which dominate the Atlantic, the decisive theatre of the war at sea. The thrusts made by our surface vessels into this theatre were operations of the greatest boldness. But now, principally as a result of the help being given to Britain by the USA, the time for such exploits is over, and the results which might be achieved do not justify the risks involved. Very soon, as the result of enemy counter-measures, our surface vessels will find themselves compelled to abandon their offensive against the enemy lines of communication in favour of the purely defensive role avoiding battle with superior enemy forces.

---

48   A situation not helped by personnel constantly being called away on active service since Nazi Germany did not use the practice of 'reserved occupation' that was enforced by the Allies, where by any occupation important for the war effort and the continuation of essential services for the running of the country were exempt from military service.

Supply by means of surface supply ship has proved impracticable.

Only the U-boat, therefore, is capable of remaining for any length of time and fighting in sea areas in which the enemy is predominant, since it alone can still carry out its operations without at the same time being compelled to accept the risk of battle against superior enemy forces. An increase in the number of enemy battleships and cruisers in these waters, far from constituting any addition to the dangers to which the U-boats are exposed, is regarded, on the contrary, as a welcome addition to the targets for which they are always searching.

For these reasons U-boat command is emphatically of the opinion that battleships and cruisers are not indispensable to the prosecution of the war in the Atlantic.

If it be also accepted that it is equally not possible to employ these ships for other purposes, such as the seizure and occupation of groups of islands, the inevitable and only logical conclusion must be that they are no longer of major importance to the prosecution of the war as a whole. That being so, maintenance personnel, which is most urgently needed for the vital U-boat arm, should no longer be wasted on the repairing of battleships and cruisers.'[49]

As if to prove Dönitz's point, in February 1942, Hitler, angry at the lack of activity on the part of the surface fleet, ordered Raeder to bring what big ships were on the Atlantic coast into Norwegian waters, the ships offering defence against his feared invasion of that coast. Raeder was opposed to this withdrawal from France as he felt it was a retreat that signified the ending of the Battle of the Atlantic, but Hitler told Raeder that unless the ships were moved, he would have them decommissioned where they lay in the French Atlantic harbour of Brest. Raeder had to comply, and in reality it was probably a good thing; with the Allies gaining aerial superiority the big ships had had their day, unless they too could sail under their own defensive umbrella of aircraft. They were not even safe where they lay with the threat from bomber aircraft ever present.

As the horrendous Baltic winter of 1941 – 42 passed, good news finally reached the *Graf Zeppelin*. On 12 March, Admiral Raeder had successfully pleaded his case with Hitler for more steel so that he could complete the carrier, highlighting how, just days before, the Führer had come close to losing his beloved battleship *Tirpitz* whilst in pursuit of an Allied convoy when she narrowly escaped torpedoes dropped by British carrier aircraft. He took the opportunity to again comment on the need for a naval air arm, and stated how ultimately the carrier still had not been completed due to a shortage of steel, the priority given to U-boat production swallowing the navy's steel allowance and necessitating the cancellation of work on the larger navy units. Hitler, convinced by Raeder's plea, immediately issued orders for the carrier to be completed 'in the shortest possible time in view of the vital importance of such a unit', stating his desire to see a German

---

49   Extract from: *Memoirs* by Karl Dönitz

naval task force composed of *Tirpitz*, *Scharnhorst*, one aircraft carrier, two heavy cruisers and 12 to 14 destroyers.

Though there were some in the naval staff who doubted the carrier's tactical value, the lifting of Admiral Raeder's May 1940 moratorium on construction of the *Graf Zeppelin* was exactly what many others within the higher echelons of the navy wanted. They believed that a carrier was the best solution to their air-cover problems and that the completion of this one ship would make it feasible to once again operate their Capital ships out in the Atlantic, at a stroke renewing the surface offensive.

With construction of the carrier about to be re-initiated, thoughts turned to the aircraft to be operated from her. Fieseler's torpedo bomber was no longer considered desirable, its inability to be catapulted partly to blame for this fall from grace. In place of the Fieselers, 28 new-generation Junker dive-bombers,[50] designation Ju 87E would be carried – replacements for the previous carrier version of this aircraft that had all been completed without their carrier attachments back in 1940 and dispatched to other squadrons. Not the most modern of aircraft, production of the Ju 87 had almost ceased altogether in 1941, but was reinstated after it became apparent that its replacement was a long way off. This new variant of the famous Stuka (derived from the Ju 87D) was capable of being catapulted while carrying a torpedo, and as a result shares in the blame for the redundant status of the Fieseler.[51] For the carrier's fighter aircraft, it was proposed to carry ten Bf 109Fs converted for shipboard duties. No longer the thoroughbred aeroplanes that had been offered three years before, the O.K.M. was not overly enamoured by either of these now outdated aircraft, but they were warned that if a new carrier aircraft were to be developed it would be 1946 before mass production of such an aircraft could be achieved.

A new fighter aircraft was requested by the navy, but in the short to medium term, due to lack of foresight on the part of both the Luftwaffe and the navy, the fighter aircraft situation was not likely to improve. As no requests for this aircraft had been made until after the March 1942 order for the re-initiation of the carrier's construction, it was to be September 1942 before Messerschmitt, at whose feet this project had been laid, got as far as completing the detailed design for this new aircraft. Designated the ME 155, at the request of the Technische Amt,[52] Messerschmitt's new aircraft was to rely heavily on existing Bf 109 parts so as to ease the manufacturer's production burden. Even so, as they had been warned, develop-

---

50   Figures for aircraft numbers vary greatly; in April at the Führer conference Hitler is talking of 22 bombers and ten fighters; by August of that year the 'K' office was furnishing Raeder with documents referring to 28 bombers and ten fighters.

51   Catapult launching for aircraft carrying torpedoes or bombs of 1000 kilograms had not previously been possible because the fixtures for attaching them to the aircraft could not withstand the strain of launching (rather than there being a problem with the aircraft itself). By 1942 improvements to these fixtures meant that catapulting was now possible.

52   Der Technische Amt was the Technical office of the State Ministry of Aviation.

ment would not happen overnight; the navy still had a considerable period of time before this new aircraft could be operational.

As for the carrier itself, with the decision to complete her now made, she would need to return to Kiel for the addition of the counterpoise bulges that are so characteristic of her in later photographs. This was easier said than done with Germany's shipyards already working flat out on U-boat production and receiving barely enough steel to meet even these demands. To top it all there was a shortage of skilled workmen, the consequence being that by July of 1942 only ten U-boats would be available for operations in the Atlantic.[53] The knock-on effect of this backlog of work was months of enforced inactivity for the carrier, which was still at Gotenhafen waiting for the order to return to Kiel for entry into the dry dock so that work could once again commence.

Caught on film by an RAF reconnaissance aircraft, proof that the Graf Zeppelin was at Gdynia. Photograph courtesy of the Imperial War Museum, London. Ref. HM5813.

Graf Zeppelin would still be at Gotenhafen on the night of 27 August 1942 when under a full moon, 12 Royal Air Force (R.A.F.) Lancaster bombers led by Guy Gibson attacked the carrier. Latest intelligence indicated that she had her crew on board, aircraft were being loaded and that she was virtually ready to sail. In reality this was far from the truth; at this point in time very few pilots had been trained to carry out the braked landings necessary for landing on a carrier's deck, and the unit selected to undergo this train-

53 Extract from: *Memoirs* by Karl Dönitz

One of the 37 mm gun emplacements installed on board the Graf Zeppelin for her journey back to Kiel.

One of the 20 mm quad guns installed on board the Graf Zeppelin for her journey back to Kiel.

ing would still be away fighting on other fronts as 1942 came to a close. *Graf Zeppelin* was spared destruction at the hands of Gibson's bomber force by a south-westerly wind which blew haze from over Berlin to the Baltic coast, reducing visibility to something like a mile, shielding her from the new 5500 lb 'capital ship bomb' for which she was a trial target. With the poor visibility over the target Gibson did not even see her, and those who did missed.

Winter was again looming when the men of Deutsche Werke (Goten-hafen branch) installed six 37 mm guns in twin mounts, 24 20 mm guns mounted in six quad fixtures and four searchlights for her protection from enemy aircraft on the journey back to Kiel. These additions not deemed necessary for the outward journey to Gotenhafen some 17 months before, were a clear demonstration of the enemy's growing ability to probe every corner of German territory.

Her long wait over, on the last day in November 1942, *Graf Zeppelin* finally slipped her moorings heading for the 40,000-ton floating dry-dock at Kiel (according to the Italian commission who visited her in Kiel later that same year, she made the journey under her own power, though other sources claim she was towed), arriving at Deutsche Werke's shipyard on 5 December. Not wanting the movements of this large and vulnerable target to be known to the Allies, whose spies and eves-droppers operated throughout the Reich, for the duration of her journey she assumed the name '*Zander*' in homage to Captain Zander who had laid the foundations for navy flying back in the 1920s.

Shortly after Hitler's March 1942 order to complete the *Graf Zeppelin* and in line with Germany's belated decision to re-embark on construction of a carrier fleet, the incomplete cruiser *Seydlitz* was designated to be fitted with a flight deck, the intention being for her to fulfil the role of an auxiliary carrier (carrying 12 bombers and six fighters), providing air cover to the Capital ships. The Führer had also ordered that the liners *Europa*, *Potsdam* and *Gneisenau* should be converted to auxiliary aircraft carriers. Allaying the Grand Admiral's fears that the Luftwaffe were dragging their feet on the issue of carrier aircraft, the Führer stated his belief that this increase in aircraft carrier numbers would simplify the mass production of carrier aircraft as they would now be needed in greater numbers.

Selected for their suitability for conversion, all these vessels met the main requirement for an auxiliary carrier, that of physical size. The criteria for auxiliary carriers as acknowledged in October 1942 by the Skl's[54] officer-in-charge of the Naval Air Section (IL) required them to be 'in an order of magnitude of around 15,000t – according to 'K'[55] this size just about allows for a productive range – incorporating speed, a large sphere of action and powerful AA guns (12 cm). It stands to reason that this type of ship will only be capable of carrying a small complement of aircraft, however the allocation of duties for this type of ship requires no large number of aircraft.'[56] Increasing that 'sphere of action', at least for the *Europa*, would come about with the planned addition of bulges similar to those *Graf Zeppelin* was destined to get, external fuel bunkers that would double as underwater protection from torpedoes and mines. The aeronautical facilities intended to be provided on board these ships, not surprisingly, were based on those available on board the *Graf Zeppelin*.

---

54 Abbreviation for 'Seekriegsleitung' the German Naval Warfare Staff. The SKL was subservient to the O.K.M.

55 'K' Not being specifically identified on this document, it would seem reasonable to presume that this was the 'Kriegsmarine Schiffsbau Büro' (K office) the department responsible for ship design and construction who had visited HMS *Furious* in 1935.

56 Taken from Raeder's personal collection that is held by the Foreign Documents Section of the Naval Historical Branch.

Aircraft carriers were high on the agenda throughout 1942, and, by May, Hitler himself was declaring it out of the question to operate the larger surface ships without carrier protection. In the absence of a carrier of their own at the start of the year the small French carrier *Joffre* was briefly considered for use as a Kriegsmarine training ship. Later, Raeder would review 'K' office specifications and data for the *Graf Zeppelin* and her planned protégé of 40,000 tons up to the largest 'Atlantic' carriers of 71,500 tons capable of deploying anything up to 100 aircraft. He would have most certainly discussed these options with the Führer at the August conference on naval affairs along with other 'K' office proposals such as a 'flying boat' carrier of 36,000 tons that was to have been approximately equal in length to the *Graf Zeppelin*. Equipped with four shafts each providing 60,000 hp and armour worthy of a battleship (250 mm side armour and two armoured decks, one of 150 mm thickness, and an upper deck of 50 mm), she was to have a proposed range of 30,000 nautical miles and carry ten BV 138 flying boats.

During this period of evaluation, the operations division of the German Naval Staff (1/Skl) carried out their own study in the attempt to alleviate what was for the navy one of the most 'salient features of Naval operations,' that of 'waging war at sea without an air arm'. Eliminating the possibility of a hybrid battleship/aircraft carrier – the 'flight-deck battleship' – as 'most unsatisfactory', they did however consider the 'flight-deck cruiser' to be viable, the staff-officer-in-charge of the Naval Air Section (IL) responding to this by declaring that it would be 'absolutely feasible to build a cruiser, which simultaneously has aircraft carrier capabilities. The problems of Start decks and Landing decks can be solved through the design and installation of improved catapult and braking systems. This type of ship would have the speed and weaponry of a cruiser and would therefore, together with its speed, armour and aircraft, be particularly suitable for its foreseeable duties of reconnaissance, anti-aircraft protection, convoy protection and trade warfare. It is plain to see that the construction of such a type of ship does not undermine the future prospects of the pure aircraft carrier, the role of the aircraft carrier with its large aircraft complement, lying mainly in the company of the large warships, thus the battleship. It is therefore unthinkable to renounce the aircraft carrier.' Acknowledging that, 'An aircraft carrier would never be capable of carrying out a major artillery battle against a battleship' and that 'the battleship, on the other hand, must and can be used for its [the aircraft carrier] protection.'[57] Though the thought of renouncing the larger carrier was deemed 'unthinkable',[58] concerns about such a valuable asset, 'whose loss, or maybe under certain circumstances simply its damage, could result in the abrupt loss of function of part or perhaps the entire air force in the area' resulted in the IL concluding that it would be more prudent to construct several smaller carriers rather than one large one, a ratio of five small carriers to each large carrier being considered far more practical.

57   Raeder document: 'aircraft carrier in the fleet formation'

58   Carrier's larger than the *Graf Zeppelin*.

For the navy, still unaided by the Luftwaffe who were either unable or unwilling to offer airborne protection for the ships and submarines that were embarking on missions, or worse, returning damaged as a result of actions with the enemy (in June 1942 only one solitary FW 200 aircraft was available for reconnaissance work, and no fighters), this period of construction offered the possibility of doing the job for themselves.

Encouraged by Hitler's new-found enthusiasm for aircraft carriers, Raeder had tried once again to establish a naval air arm, drawing up the following memorandum for a Führer conference: 'The order has been given to complete the carrier *Graf Zeppelin*, and to convert the cruiser *Seydlitz* and so far three merchant ships into auxiliary carriers. Under favourable working conditions the Navy will thereby acquire five additional front line units by the end of 1944 or early 1945. Through their assignment for reconnaissance and offensive operations the airplanes aboard these carriers become an instrument of naval warfare. The Air Force units which will then be part of the Navy will be so strong in personnel as well as material, that a new line of demarcation will have to be drawn between Navy and Air Force interests with regard to the personnel and ground organisation. The Naval Staff therefore considers the creation of a Fleet Air Arm essential. With the organisation of this Fleet Air Arm the ship plane squadron could revert from the Air Force command back to the Navy. The future Fleet Air Arm would then be composed of carrier and ship plane squadrons. They would operate under the over-all command of the Navy high command. Administrative jurisdiction would be exercised by the fleet command. Training and operation would be carried out by an admiral of the Fleet Air Arm under the Fleet command.' Enthusiastic or not, Hitler replied that he believed it to be impossible to build up this naval air force with the war still going on.

At this time the carrier era must have seemed tantalisingly close to all concerned, landings on a flight deck were well practiced, some of the trials at the Travemünde Experimental Centre being witnessed in November 1941 by the visiting Italian commission who were taken to an 'airfield laid out for landing'. They described a 'circular asphalt platform 40 meters in diameter – the brake wire is fixed across the circle diametrically and can be moved, according to the direction of the wind. The lateral limits of the flight deck are represented by strips of wood….'. On board the ship it was intended that there would be four brake wires stretched across the flight deck as a safeguard against an aircraft bouncing over the first,[59] but in 1941 these were not yet actually in place. Describing the demonstrations observed at the Travemünde Experimental Centre, the report goes on to say, 'The brake capstan is contained in a pit. Nothing projects above ground level except the system of pulleys for the retrieving of the rope [the word 'rope' referring to the steel brake cable] and the apparatus for regulating it.

The rope is also brought back to the capstan from the other side of the ground

---

59 A fifth wire was also being considered for installation instead of having a safety net at the end of the landing-on area as originally considered.

via a gallery. Thus, for landing purposes, the ground has the same dimensions and exigencies as the flying deck except that it has one rope only instead of four.

The electric power for working the brake is supplied by moveable motor generators placed at the edge of the platform.

The commission watched a dozen braked landings made by Heinkel 50, Fieseler 167 and Junkers 87 A/c; some made by the A/c simply taxying [sic], others with a regular landing within the limits of the airfield. The braking process appears smooth and gradual: the tail of the plane is raised, but not enough for the propeller to touch the ground. Sometimes the hook did not work because the pilot, who was a new pupil, had forgotten to lower the catch; twice, on the other hand, although the catch had been lowered the hook jumped the wire and the braking was not effected. With four wires as on the real flight deck it is considered that it will be impossible for more than one of them to be jumped.'[60]

At the time of the commission's 1941 visit 'several thousand' landings had been carried out, without fatality. When the commission returned late the following year, the solitary brake winch that was being evaluated at Travemünde had stopped somewhere in the region of 3500 aircraft, many with just the auxiliary mechanical brake and was still in good working order. By this second visit in December of 1942, much had been done to ensure the safe braking of aircraft on the carrier's deck. Accelerometers placed inside the aircraft measured the deceleration of the aircraft when it hooked the arrestor cable. Coupled with filmed footage of these landings braking was facilitated in such away that would help minimise the risk of the aircraft turning over at the end of the run, and yet still stop a Bf 109 returning at 140 kmh in less than 33 metres, while smaller, lighter craft could be halted in less than 16 metres. As if to demonstrate the thoroughness of the research, the Italian commission were taken by their German hosts to the Experimental Centre at Travemünde, where they spoke with engineers and were shown footage of a 'long series of braked landings carried out by Fi.167, He.50, Arado 197, Arado 96, Ju.87, Me.109 aircraft' of which it was noted that there was a tendency for the 'aircraft's tail to rise at the end of the run.'[61] The series then goes

---

60   National Archive document: ADMT 19137

61   Though no longer intending to use them from the carrier, Arado's Ar. 96, 195, 197 and Heinkel's He. 50 were used to practice flight deck landings at the Travemünde Experimental Centre. The He.50 in particular was popular as a training aircraft due to its slow landing speed (90 kmh) and ease of manoeuvering. The Ar. 96 had been commissioned in 1936 (ahead of the laying of the keel for carrier 'A') as a torpedo bomber and reconnaissance aircraft for shipboard use and came with folding wings to aid storage. An unsuccessful aircraft, it was superseded by the Ar. 195 which was itself a failure owing to its low performance in comparison with Fieseler's aircraft the Fi.167 - which was of course originally selected for use on the carrier. The Ar. 197 was designed as a shipboard fighter but lack of support from the Luftwaffe meant its development was slow, development of the aircraft being stopped before the end of 1937 when it became apparent that it was already outdated. Heinkel's He.50 was exported to Japan in the mid-1930s as the He.66 and later, after some modifications produced there under licence by Aichi as the D1A1-type 94 carrier bomber, operating from Japan's aircraft carriers until the early 1940's. It also served in Germany's first dive-bomber unit that was formed in 1935. - *Warplanes of the Third Reich*, William Green.

on to show the 'First experiments of taking off and landing on the flight-deck of a ship of medium tonnage (aircraft Fieseler 'storch').

Mooring and buoyancy tests with model A/C [aircraft] in a tank and with real A/C.

Tests of braked-landings with Me.109, Arado 197, He.50, Fi.167, Ju.87 A/C. In this film several landing accidents are recorded due to initial nosing down of the A/C with consequent deformation of the propeller'.[62]

Besides creating a safe aircraft braking system for the carrier, this research had also demonstrated a need for the first wire of the brake to be moved further along the deck, creating more of a platform behind it. Initially only 28 metres from the stern it was now intended to install this first wire 50 metres

The 'landing brake' and 'ropes' that a returning aircraft would have to snag with it's tail hook.

in, each subsequent wire being evenly spaced at ten or 12 metre intervals.

Built by Demag (Deutsche Maschinenfabrik A.G. Duisburg) the brakes were improved versions of those operated by the Japanese on board their carriers. Demag's version had been improved so as to include an auxiliary mechanical brake that would allow the equipment to be operated in the event of the power supply failing (though due to the heat generated it was advised that, 'not more than 7 or 8 consecutive braking operations [should be] undertaken'). The brake consisted of two drums connected to a single capstan from which the brake wire ran, all of which was to be housed below the flight deck. Of the brake itself, all that would be visible, suspended approximately 20 cm above the flight deck, was the steel cable, 22 mm in diameter, there in position to be snagged by the retractable hook protruding 40 cm below the tail wheel of the landing carrier aircraft. The brake wire would run from one drum, up over the flight deck and back to be wound onto the other drum. When the wire was caught and dragged by a landing aircraft it would force the two drums to turn, the capstan acting as

62   National Archive document: ADMT 19137

a brake and stopping the aircraft. Allowing for the resetting of the equipment, it would be possible for an aircraft to land every two minutes.

Incredibly, the biggest stumbling block the *Graf Zeppelin* now faced before she could be declared ready for operations was not the construction of the counterpoise bulges, but the need for more substantial equipment for the operation of her aircraft. Weighing in excess of six tons, the new Junker was considerably heavier than the originally converted Ju 87B, and would cause a problem for the brake winches, as these were only rated for a five-ton aircraft. As the elevators were also only rated for a five-ton aircraft, they too would need attention. She was also in need of some trials to be carried out on her engine-room machinery and boilers. Her accommodation areas were yet to be fully fitted and amongst other things the aircraft fuelling system was not yet fully installed and of course all of her artillery was still absent, though by now the heavier weapons were of dubious necessity. The increased weight of the designated aircraft would also cause a problem for the catapult system that may have required its replacement. To construct, test and bring into service a new catapult was expected to take up to two years, though if the existing equipment could be converted, this could be reduced to 18 months.[63]

The construction of the counterpoise bulges that had necessitated *Graf Zeppelin*'s entry into the dry dock at Kiel were intended to compensate for a list of 4°30' that the carrier developed when she was fully loaded.[64] It had been considered possible to correct the list by consumption of fuel oil but this would have taken some 100 hours of steaming, an excessive time and one in which landing of aircraft could easily be affected. Even though it was considered possible for an aircraft to land with a role of up to four or five degrees, this is a state that would easily be reached in a rough sea with a bit of a swell, when the decks are already sloping in excess of four degrees. However, the bulges, being symmetrical, were not enough in themselves to correct the list. This would be achieved by:

a) **The addition of 300 tons of solid, fixed ballast.**
b) **Varying the thickness of the plates of the bulges, those on the port side being 35 mm, while on the starboard side it was only 12 mm.**
c) **Distribution of the weights of supplies.**

Though not quite the anti-roll system originally intended for the ship, the bulges could be used to hold some 120 tons of water in the event of battle damage.

---

63 A delay that could have been avoided, the catapult equipment was not critical to the operation of the ship, it being perfectly possible for the aircraft to take off in a conventional manner; 170m of flight deck were available for this (as had been the intention for the Fieseler and some of the Stuka aircraft, and as had been advised by the Japanese whose carriers were not fitted with catapults).

64 In the National Archive document: ADMT 19137, there is a claim that this list was to port, but the fact that the port-side bulges were thicker and thus heavier would suggest otherwise. Some sources claim this list resulted from a taller funnel being added and armoured command and weapons control being built on. The truth is probably a combination of both.

Graf Zeppelin in the 40,000 ton floating dry dock at Kiel. Her new counterpoise bulges are clearly visible. Bundesarchiv RM 25 Bild-64

Pumped through the huge 500 mm double sluice valves in less than a minute to the necessary side of the ship, this water could be used to correct up to a 2° list, a further 7° being correctable by the movement of other liquids onboard the ship, though this would take considerably longer at 15–20 minutes. This system could be used in port to assist in the loading and unloading of munitions when the absence of any list whatsoever was desirable. Fixed to the bottom of the existing bilge keels and divided horizontally into two separate tanks these bulges could also be used to increase her endurance by doubling as external fuel tanks and increasing her range by 1500 miles. As an added bonus, by only filling these tanks to three-quarters full they would still provide some underwater protection from mines and torpedoes.

For the duration of her time at Kiel *Graf Zeppelin* would have not only had the protection of the smoke generating equipment that completely surrounded Kiel bay with units being placed every 50 metres, but would also lie under her own camouflage. The visiting Italian commission, there to see the German carrier as part of an ongoing partnership to help with their own incomplete carrier the HIMS *Aquila*, described how as part of this camouflage two wooden trellis work platforms ten metres high were erected on her deck both forward and aft of the superstructure. Indeed, it was common practice to change the outline of a ship by means of these wooden constructions. The platforms themselves remaining uncamouflaged, the hull of the ship could be made to disappear (at least from the air) with the aid of galvanised steel nets covered in tassels that danced in the wind, giving the appearance of shimmering water. The illusion would be made to merge with its background by the continuation of the tassel-covered netting over the vessel's decks and onto the quay on one side and across to a series of floats anchored in the harbour on the other.

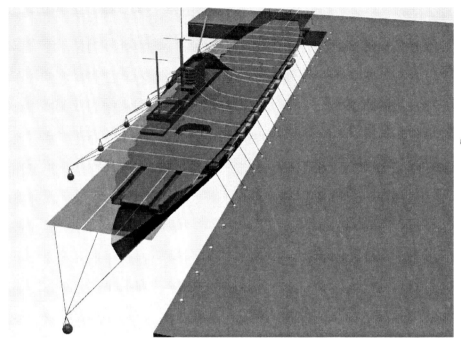

How Graf Zeppelin would have looked under the camouflaged netting used to hide her during her time at Kiel

Protection was provided from falling ordinance, aimed or otherwise at the ship moored alongside the quay by anti-bomb protective netting. Constructed of steel cable and secured from the deck of the ship onto the harbour wall, this netting was intended to divert a bomb onto the quay and would help ensure that no bomb could land in the gap between harbour and ship doing more damage than was due from such a device.

Germany's carrier fleet seemingly once again on the rise must have been an exciting prospect for the Kriegsmarine, whose battleships had withdrawn earlier that year from the besieged harbours they occupied along France's Atlantic coast – harbours which were under constant surveillance from British submarines and aircraft, and from which virtually no vessel's departure went un-noted. *Graf Zeppelin* and the smaller 'auxiliary' carriers operating from these Biscay ports could provide fighter cover and reconnaissance for surface units and cargo vessels, just as the British escort carriers had been doing since 1941,[65] or could operate as raiders in their own right, with their own aircraft seeking out and attacking Allied shipping.

---

65 HMS *Audacity* escorted several convoys from September of 1941; though lost to a German U-boat before the year was out, she had proved a resounding success, her aircraft playing an important role in the sinking of a several U-boats and the shooting down of seven Focke Wolf Kondors that had been operating as bombers and reconnaissance aircraft, shadowing the patrol and homing in other vessels for the attack. (Reference: www.royalnavyresearcharchive.org.uk)

The Turning Tide

THE BEGINNING OF THE END

The 1942 visit by Italy's naval commission gives an interesting insight into the carrier's level of completion. They would report, 'The progress of the work on the ship was found to be at precisely the same stage as described by the preceding mission, a little over twelve months before, namely: the hull completely in position, engines and boilers ready to function although all trials had not yet been carried out. The electrical plant is complete except for the cables of some small supply units. The artillery installations are entirely lacking, the electrical connections for them appear to be prepared. The equipment of the living quarters is yet to be finished. The hangar lifts are ready. The petrol system is in process of being fitted. The covering of the parts of the ship relating to artillery and the small items of equipment is lacking. The navigational fittings are all ready. Furthermore, the ship has sailed under her own steam at least from STETTIN, where she was last visited, to Kiel.

The impression is given that she is 85 per cent ready.

At present she is in dock for work on the counterpoise bulges, which has not, yet begun, as there were no workmen aboard.

The reason for the suspension of work was asked for and the answer given was, that for the time being the workmen were employed elsewhere on urgent tasks.

Probably urgent tasks meant the construction of Submarines, because only Submarines are under construction at Kiel, as we were able to confirm while crossing the Deutsch-Werke [sic] shipyards.

Roughly 20 were under construction' (the carrier had of course been the last steamship launched at Kiel before U-boat construction began).

Interestingly, even at this period of prolific aircraft carrier construction (five were now undergoing construction/conversion) the visiting commission would observe that, 'The impression was however received that the principal reason for the delay in completion was the lack of urgency due to friction between Air Force and Navy concerning the allocation of personnel to the training centre… The Navy says there is no hurry to get the ship ready because training [of the aircrew] ashore has not yet begun and therefore they are sure to be in time whenever this training begins.

The Air Force at TRAVEMUNDE says that as the ship is not ready there is plenty of time.

The truth must be that aircraft carriers are of no great interest for immediate purposes, but an impression was received that disagreements also exist between the Navy and the Air Force.' [66]

Just a few weeks after this visit, Hitler's enthusiasm for a German naval task force ended. On 6 January 1943, he ordered all the heavy navy units out of action, proposing that their guns be removed and installed as shore emplacements. As for the aircraft carriers, Hitler went on to ask Raeder to evaluate if those undergoing construction should be retained and if so, could the navy also evaluate the possibility of converting some of the heavy units he was withdrawing from service into more carriers?

This sudden desire to convert the battleships into carriers was no doubt partly the doing of Herman Göring. He had been present with Hitler at his headquarters while he (Hitler) had been anxiously waiting for word of the overdue ships *Hipper*, *Lützow* (formerly *Deutschland*) and their accompanying destroyers that had sailed under the command of Admiral Kummetz against an enemy convoy. Always keen to highlight the failures of the other services, Göring preyed on Hitler's anxieties muttering about the ineffectiveness of the navy's big ships.

Perhaps it was Göring who had first suggested converting the battleships into carriers. He was after all under increasing pressure to produce a significant number of aircraft for the *Graf Zeppelin* and those ships that were undergoing carrier conversion. If the Kriegsmarine surface fleet were to now convert to a purely aircraft carrier orientated force, devoid of other capital ships, the fleet would virtually belong to him.

This latest furore had arisen when, having heard nothing of the fate of *Hipper* and *Lützow* except for a report broadcast on Britain's BBC news claiming that they had been involved in an unsuccessful action in which they had been driven off, Hitler flew into a rage. In an audience with Raeder he ranted at the Grand Admiral in a mammoth hour and a half monologue, scorning the navy and everything it had ever done declaring 'the big ships were utterly worthless and could not do anything without air cover and smaller ships as escorts.'[67] When Hitler finished, Raeder asked for the other officers present to leave the room and immediately offered his resignation. Though Hitler tried to convince him to stay, declaring that the smaller ships of the fleet did good work, Raeder was not prepared to see his life's work undone, having seen the fleet rise again after World War I he would not destroy it. Feeling his authority had been questioned, and

66   National Archive document: ADMT 19137

67   Extract from: *Grand Admiral* by Erich Raeder

pointing out that he was now 67 years of age and not in the best of health, he agreed to stay until the end of the month, 30 January being his tenth anniversary as Commander in Chief under Hitler which would seem to the public and the world at large a natural time for him to leave.[68]

By the time of Raeder's departure, Hitler had heard the truth of Kummetz's mission. Far from the failure described by the BBC, *Hipper* and *Lützow* had actually sunk a couple of British destroyers and damaged another for the loss of just one of their own destroyers and a hit to *Hipper's* boiler room: Not a dazzling victory, but certainly not the failure Hitler thought. Correctly maintaining radio silence, Admiral Kummetz had withdrawn to Alta Fjord sending a message when he arrived. Unbeknown to him, a failure in the landlines in northern Norway meant the report by the BBC was the first to be heard by the anxious Hitler, as ever restless for information about his ships. Whatever the outcome of Kummetz's mission, Raeder's resignation still stood, and in its aftermath Hitler had the following order circulated, but only to certain selected officers 'on account of the psychological effect':

1. All work in progress on heavy ships now building or in process of conversion is to cease forthwith.
2. All battleships, armoured ships and cruisers other than those needed for training purposes are to be placed in reserve.
3. Naval personnel, workmen, etc., who become available as a result of this directive are to be employed with a view to accelerating the building and repair of U-boats.

The order to stop work on the *Graf Zeppelin* arrived on 2 February, construction work being brought to a halt on the other ships in Germany's planned carrier fleet of less than a year before at about the same time.[69]

Seydlitz had progressed as far as the removal of her artillery and the cutting off of her superstructure and funnel; the conversion of the liners had not fared any better.

In his last month as Grand Admiral, Raeder was not idle. Days after he issued his resignation, in a memorandum to Hitler he would try to reverse the Führer's decision to scrap the fleet, explaining calmly the importance of a balanced fleet of carriers, battleships and cruisers etc., and how the 'fleet in being' could hold captive an equal number of Royal Navy Capital ships, thus relieving other theatres of the menace of these ships. He went on to say, 'The lack of adequate air forces for reconnaissance and cover and the fact that it has not proved possible to add air power in the shape of aircraft carriers to the fighting powers of the

---

68 Raeder's departure, by chance, would be overshadowed by the capitulation of General Paulus and the 6th Army, encircled after the failure of Stalingrad, 94,000 men being taken prisoner.

69 This suspension of work also ended development on the Me.155, the carrier-borne fighter aircraft under development by Messerschmitt as a replacement for the aging Bf 109 (a.k.a. the Me.109).

ships themselves have, since the spring of 1942, imposed sharp limitations on the manner in which the naval High Command could employ the fleet as a corporate entity and have acted as a drag on prospects of achieving success.

On the other hand I must point out that the possibility of scoring a success most certainly still exists, provided that the fleet remains constantly on the alert for every possible contingency and waits for the favourable opportunity. Even without adequate air cover and reconnaissance, opportunities will always occur when, by making full use of favourable weather conditions, we can achieve surprise and strike a worthwhile blow.' Still Hitler refused to change his mind; he did though take Raeder's recommendation for his successor as Grand Admiral. With both Admiral Carls and Dönitz being nominated by Raeder as suitable candidates for the role, Hitler would choose Dönitz (who was the head of the U-boat arm), perhaps an indication of the move away from surface warfare.

Raeder's final act would be to once more try to spare the Capital ships. Addressing Dönitz, '[Raeder] once more emphasised that the Capital ships could be employed in the Arctic, but that if the fleet went into action, it must do so unhampered by any political restrictions, which forbade it, for reasons of prestige, to risk incurring any losses.'[70]

On taking command Dönitz immediately showed his mettle, and within the month had done what Raeder could not; he got Hitler to reverse his decision. Though originally drawing up plans to scrap the fleet as Hitler had ordered, he (Dönitz) 'very quickly realised, however, that I should have to examine the whole question of this paying off and scrapping of the big ships once again and thoroughly. As a result of further scrutiny I came to the conclusion that withdrawing these ships from service would not result in any appreciable increase in either manpower or material and the implementation of the project could not but react politically and militarily to our disadvantage. Breaking them up was an even less attractive solution for it made considerable claims on labour and technical resources.

Thus for the same reason as my predecessor, I came to the conclusion that Hitler's order was wrong. On February 26, I reported to him in this sense – Hitler grudgingly agreed.'[71] Dönitz did however agree that some of the older ships and those that were no longer of any value should be laid up, these being the cruisers *Hipper, Leipzig, Köln* and the old battleships *Schleswig-Holstein* and *Schlesien*. The work on the *Graf Zeppelin*'s counterpoise bulges was however to continue.

Of all the ships that Dönitz had been able to retain for the navy, his insistence on maintaining the *Graf Zeppelin* may well have 'stood on the toes' of Raeder's old rival Hermann Göring. Perhaps taking advantage of Hitler's lack of faith in the ability of the Kriegsmarine High Command

---

70   Extract from: *Memoirs* by Karl Dönitz

71   Extract from: *Memoirs* by Karl Dönitz

(O.K.M.[72]) to operate its big ships, it would appear that Göring, after years of showing little interest in maritime affairs, had had his eye on Germany's largest floating asset. Just nine days after the decision by Hitler to withdraw the heavier ships of the fleet that had culminated in Raeder's resignation, Göring's Chief of Air Staff issued the following order to the 'Fliegerführer Afrika':

...FULLY TRAINED STUKA PILOTS WITH BLIND FLYING CERTIFICATE 1 ARE TO BE SUPPLIED BY THE STUKA UNITS FOR THE CARRIER GRAF ZEPPELIN, AND SENT TO PAROW + BY 1/3/43. THE GRUPPE WILL NOMINATE BY RETURN TO THE GESCHWADER 1 PILOT (NAME, CHRISTIAN NAME, RANK, WHETHER OR NOT IN POSSESSION OF BLIND-FLYING CERTIFICATE 1) IF THE PILOT IS NOT YET IN POSSESSION OF BLIND-FLYING CERTIFICATE 1, HE WILL BE TRAINED BY DIRECTOR OF TRAINING BY 1/3/43.[73]

A close confidante of Hitler, by the time this order was issued Göring would undoubtedly have already known about Hitler's decision on the fate of the heavy ships, and Raeder's resulting resignation. Could it be that these two events were the catalyst for an attempt to requisition the partially finished carrier for the Luftwaffe? Or that Göring saw an opportunity to expand his empire and instructed his Chief of Air Staff to act? It would certainly seem feasible and lends some credence to the suggestion that the idea of converting the big ships into carriers originated from Göring. *Graf Zeppelin* would have been a very desirable addition to the numerous seaplane tenders that the Luftwaffe already operated, the pilots sent by the Fliegerführer Afrika staking a claim for the Luftwaffe on the carrier.

Göring could have seen to the releasing of these men for service with the navy at any time, but he didn't, his lack of aerial support during three and a half years of war needlessly sacrificing many sailors' lives. The timing of the decision to furnish the navy with aircrews just as the larger naval vessels were ordered out of action, and the carrier's future was in doubt, can be seen as nothing more than a vain attempt to increase Luftwaffe prestige as the dominant German force at sea. It would not have mattered to Göring that the North African campaign from which these aircrews were being summoned was already struggling. Even the loss of Tripoli to the Allies just two months after this order was issued and the subsequent loss of North Africa just four months later would have been of little concern to the Reichsmarschall (Göring), for tactical considerations were never a factor in these circumstances, rather Göring's desire for power and self-importance. However, whatever Göring and his Chief of Staff's motive had been for

72 German abbreviation for 'Ober Kommando der Marine'

73 The National Archives HW1319

recalling these aircrews, the *Graf Zeppelin* stayed in naval hands.

After streamlining the fleet Dönitz then looked inwards at the naval organisation. He must have been horrified to find that the navy, unlike the Luftwaffe, had no representative sitting on the Central Planning Committee – the organisation responsible for the allocation of steel. Dönitz discovered that whereas the Luftwaffe would request and then argue via its representative on the committee for its materials, the navy simply submitted its requests in writing and then waited for the scraps to fall from the committee's table, the result being that their requests were never met in full. The navy's lack of representation on this committee had ensured that by 1942, even though German steel production had increased during the course of the war, the navy's steel allocation had actually fallen by more than 40,000 tons per month.[74] The result was that U-boat production suffered, being nearly three boats per month behind the planned twenty-two and a half. Other vessels such as patrol boats, E-boats, destroyers etc. suffered even more so, their production being down by some 46 per cent. Dönitz pointed out, 'Solely in order to carry out the 1943 building programme – apart altogether from the increase in Naval construction which I intended to make...our allocation had to be increased by 60,000 tons to 181,000. Even if this requirement were met in full, it would still represent only 6.4% of the country's total steel production....' Perhaps demonstrating some of the failings of the old Grand Admiral, whose lack of appetite for political involvement had left the navy absent from the central planning committee, Dönitz had his request answered, and an increase was granted. 'On March 6, 1943, he [Hitler] directed that the navy should in future receive an additional 45,000 tons per month. This at least meant that our allocation would suffice for the most pressing of our needs.'

Another situation that Raeder had tolerated was the draft of skilled workmen into the armed forces to be replaced by unskilled men requiring training. The drafting of these men resulted in a shortage of skilled workers and meant the construction of new ships and submarines took a long time, as did repairs to damaged shipping. In little more than a week after his appointment Dönitz secured an exemption for his men from military service.

In March, the new Grand Admiral reciprocated the Italian visit of late 1942. Keen to give the Supermarina (Italy's naval force) 'every possible assistance' in their flagging Mediterranean war, he flew to Rome to confer with Admiral Riccardi, his opposite number in the Supermarina. Arriving on 17 March, Dönitz was rewarded with a visit to the Palazzo Venezia in accompaniment with Admiral Riccardi for an audience with Mussolini. However, despite assistance given to Supermarina, directly from Kriegsmarine vessels in the defence of the all-important Tunisian convoys supplying German and Italian forces in North Africa, and indirectly with techno-

---

74   At the start of the war the navy received an average of 160,000 tons of steel per month.

logical assistance bidding to increase Supermarina offensive capabilities,[75] North Africa fell to the Allies. Suffering greatly at the hands of the Royal Navy, between his commission's last visit to the *Graf Zeppelin* in December 1942 and the ending of Axis resistance in Tunisia in the spring of the following year, Admiral Riccardi had lost 28 destroyers and torpedo boats with another 62 suffering damage.[76]

The situation in the Mediterranean was hopeless. Before long Sicily would be invaded by the Allies and just weeks later Mussolini resigned. Dönitz's mission to Rome had been a waste of time. Italy, whose officers and men just months before had walked the decks of the *Graf Zeppelin*, long before this year was over would be an enemy of the Reich, fighting side by side with Great Britain and her allies. The passage through the Mediterranean unobstructed, supplies for Soviet troops would flow unhampered via the Suez Canal to the Persian Gulf and then onwards overland to these troops, who themselves in turn headed west towards the Reich.

Anticipating Italy's surrender in the wake of Mussolini's departure from office, Hitler and his staff had quickly planned and then instigated the installation of a puppet Fascist government again led by Mussolini. Supported by German troops, as Southern Italy surrendered to the Allies, central and northern Italy were seized for the Fascist regime. As part of this occupation, Germany attempted to seize the Italian fleet, but was only partially successful and some of the ships escaped to the Allies, the battleship *Roma* being sunk by German aircraft as she fled. As for the Italian carrier *Aquila*, though moored in the Fascist controlled north, she remained unfinished, her completion being further delayed by the actions of saboteurs who ensured that Germany would gain nothing for their time and technology invested in this ship. Attempts to repair her were dashed when she was further damaged in air raids that ensured she never saw active service.

Even with the surface area of Hitler's empire in terminal decline, the flow of men and munitions still continued to flow to the Fronts, though not unhampered by the ever-increasing number of air raids targeted against the industrial areas, railroads and docklands of Germany. Although Kiel would come under increasingly intense aerial attacks, it was still very much operational when *Graf Zeppelin* had departed on 21 April after the completion of her new counterpoise bulges for the two-day journey to a mooring on the Mönne River (a branch of the Öder near Stettin). *Graf Zeppelin*'s move to her Stettin home of 1941, though not safe, was certainly a better choice than staying in Kiel, which by the war's end would be 'in a state of indescribable chaos, completely out of action, with 80-90 per cent of buildings destroyed and every building having suffered damage. Of the 10,000

---

75   For example, shared technical drawings and surplus aircraft carrier parts such as catapults, and aircraft arrestor equipment (brakes) built for the now long since dismantled *Peter Straßer*, to aid completion of the Italian carrier *Aquila*.

76   Extract from: *Der Seekrieg* by Friedrich Ruge.

employees who had worked [there] only a handful remained.'[77]

Though Dönitz had opted to complete the construction work being carried out on the carrier, for now she did not feature in his battle plan. The decision to relocate the *Graf Zeppelin* to Stettin was without doubt influenced by the now greatly limited supply of heavy fuel oil needed for her numerous, thirsty, oil-fired boilers.[78] Acute shortages of manpower that by this point in the war plagued the Kriegsmarine must have been another consideration. Requiring nearly one and a half thousand men to operate this one vessel – enough to crew approximately 30 U-boats – plus crew for the numerous escort vessels that would be needed as companions for her, Dönitz chose to put her in reserve.

Now more complete and more seaworthy than ever, even if the numerous men, materials and aircraft needed to commission *Graf Zeppelin* were to become available, she would soon be lacking a task force to sail with. In September of 1943, the *Tirpitz* was put out of action by mines planted underneath her by the mini submarine *X-6*. Carrying two mines, each consisting of over one and a half tons of Amatex high explosive, *X-6* did considerable damage to *Tirpitz's* propellers and steering gear. It was as a result of the damage *Tirpitz* sustained in this attack that the *Scharnhorst* (her sister *Gneisenau* having been decommissioned the previous year after massive damage caused during an air raid on Kiel) would be operating alone in pursuit of an Allied convoy when she stumbled into what became known as the Battle of the North Cape. Cornered by HMS *Duke of York* and numerous other Royal Navy ships, *Scharnhorst* never stood a chance; she was lost on 26 December with only 36 members from her crew of over 2000 men surviving.

From 1944 what was left of the Capital ships now operated in the Baltic, and though Soviet Russia may have been victorious in the bloody land battles that were raging, claims that they were impeding 'German Supreme Command in the use of its warships' were simply not true. As late as October 1944 *Lützow* and *Prinz Eugen*, in spite of repeated attacks by aircraft, were able to provide heavy artillery support against Russian troops trying to reach the Baltic port of Memel. *Lützow* and *Prinz Eugen* were instrumental in maintaining German command of Memel[79] until February of 1945 allowing for the evacuation of troops and the re-supply of the port's defenders.

The 30 January 1945, the twelfth anniversary of Hitler coming to power and the second since the surrender of Paulus and the 6th Army, brought great tragedy to the freezing cold waters of the Baltic, when the Russian submarine *S-13* torpedoed and sunk the liner *Wilhelm Gustloff* which was

---

77   BIOS report p. 43 (Imperial War Museum collection, Duxford).

78   Though fuel oil was in short supply, diesel, as used by U-boats and the pocket battleships, was much more abundant.

79   Extract from: *Der Seekrieg* by Friedrich Ruge.

involved in the exodus of some of the 2.2 million people, both soldiers and civilians, who would flee over the water from advancing Russian troops during the four months of the war in 1945. Nobody really knows how many people died when the *Wilhelm Gustloff* sunk, but conservative estimates put it at over 6000 men, women and children.

Less than a fortnight later, *S-13* struck again, again at a liner, again with huge loss of life, the loss of the *General Von Steuben* adding approximately 3000 souls to the *Gustloff*'s tragedy.

Before the war ended *S-13* would claim another 6000 deaths, with the sinking of the transport *Goya*.[80] This was not the mastery of the seas proclaimed by the Soviets, and in reality was only a small percentage of the ships daily running back and forth between the Baltic ports carrying fleeing refugees until the final day of the war.

The larger units of the Kriegsmarine active until the end went unmolested by Russia's 'Red Banner Fleet'. Offering support to its troops right up until April, the Kriegsmarine only ceased operations when lack of fuel, a problem that had been prevalent since late 1941, meant the Battle group had to withdraw. It has been speculated that the Red Banner Fleet was saving itself for the coming 'peace', hoping to emerge from the ravages of war intact and ready to face the west.

On 30 March 1945, as the Soviet Army advanced towards Berlin along the Baltic coast, taking Gotenhafen, on a path that would inevitably lead it past Stettin barely 80 miles away from the German capital, where nearly two years the carrier had lain inactive, Supreme Head Quarters of the Armed Forces issued Hitler's scorched earth policy. The policy stated that no demolition of harbours or dockyard facilities was to take place without Dönitz's permission, but when permission was received they should deal with 'the whole of this question in my name as they saw fit'. So it was, on 25 April 1945, five days before Hitler's suicide and Dönitz's succession as Führer, with the Red Army in view,[81] Captain Wolfgang Kähler ensured that they would not take the carrier intact. Kähler, at one time Captain of the *Gneisenau*, had been heavily involved with the evacuation of the Russian Front. As Commander of the *Emden* it was he who had seen to the loading of President Otto Von Hindenburg's remains onto the *Emden*'s deck for evacuation from his Prussian mausoleum, preventing them from falling into Russian hands, and it was he, who in an act reminiscent of 1919 and the defiant scuttling of Germany's High Seas Fleet, ordered the scuttling of the *Graf Zeppelin*. Explosive charges, rigged throughout the ship were detonated; the blasts decimated her turbine room, electrical installations and almost inverted her elevators, the actual sinking the result of numerous perforations in her hull.

---

80   Extract from: *Der Seekrieg* by Friedrich Ruge.

81   The Red Army, having been in the Stettin area for quite some time by now had arrived at the Altdamm Bridge, a crossing of the Öder River, several weeks before, an intense action having been fought there.

What should have been Raeder's crowning glory in the opening years of the 1940s, the *Graf Zeppelin*, a ship that could have changed the course of history, with a mere half a metre under her keel settled almost imperceptibly into the Mönne River and obscurity.

Carrier Operations

LIFE ON BOARD A NAZI CARRIER—BASED ON KRIEGSMARINE OPERATING PLANS FOR THE GRAF ZEPPELIN

In recognition of their role as a primary source of protection for the carrier, and the intention for them to be launched exclusively by catapult, had the *Graf Zeppelin* ever been completed, her fighter aircraft would have been stored in the forward portion of the upper hangar mounted on their launching trolleys. From here it was known to take less than three minutes to get the aircraft from the warm comfort of the hangar maintained at 25°C onto the elevator and secured onto one of the two traction wires of the telescopic catapults that were embedded in the perpetually windy flight deck (in tests using a real aircraft on a full-scale wooden mock-up of the elevator and hangar arrangements it was done in two minutes and 20 seconds an additional safety factor of 40 seconds being added).

To help with the manoeuvring of the aircraft within the confines of the hangar, a second trolley known as the transport trolley was used. Intended purely for use within the hangar, once the aircraft had been pushed and pulled by the hangar crew over to the lowered elevator this transport trolley would have been removed so as to drop the aircraft, already mounted on a launching trolley, onto a railed section of the elevator. Once the elevator had ascended to the flight deck the aircraft's engine would be started by compressed air allowing the machine to taxi forward, guided by the elevator's rails onto one of the two catapult tracks; the launching trolley would latch onto the traction wire of the catapult via a sprung mechanism halfway along its length.

Once extended each catapult could deploy eight aircraft, plus a test run at speeds of up to 140 kmh, allowing, when used alternately, an aircraft every 30 seconds to take off, after which the compressed air cylinders that provided the power to the catapult would need recharging, a process that took 50 minutes. During the recharging of the catapults' compressed air tanks, it would of course still be possible for aircraft to take to the skies under their own power by utilising the 170 metres of flight deck forward of the fourth arrestor wire dedicated to this type of take-off. Aircraft making a running take-off would arrive on deck via the mid-ship's elevator, the same elevator that would be used to strike aircraft back below decks upon their return. However, for aircraft carrying heavier payloads such as torpedoes, 170 metres would not give a long enough run to safely get airborne; they would need the extra deck space given by starting from much further aft, arriving upon deck via the aft-most elevator, inconveniently located in the middle of the landing area.

When the order came in 1942 to resume construction of the carrier, developments in catapulting technology had already spelt the end for the Fi 167 aircraft. Designed especially for carrier operations and at one time destined to be the most numerous aircraft onboard the ship (it being intended to carry 20), the Fi 167's inability to be catapulted meant it was no longer considered potential equipment for Germany's sole carrier,[82] its numbers being replaced by the Ju 87. Capable of taking off with or without catapult assistance when operating in the role of dive-bomber, after some initial difficulties the Ju 87 also proved capable of being catapulted when carrying a torpedo[83] and thus gaining the favour of the O.K.M. was selected as the sole carrier aircraft to fulfil the role of bomber/torpedo aircraft.

The Fieseler's ability to hang virtually stationary over a spot and to land in a very short distance[84] like the most famous Fieseler aircraft, the 'Storch', would have benefited it greatly in reconnaissance and smoke-laying roles (originally two of these aircraft were to be stored in the upper hangar deck as dedicated smoke-laying aircraft[85]). The extraordinary ability that this aircraft possessed could almost make a case for maintaining a smaller number of them on board the carrier for these roles. However, logic would dictate the better performance of the Ju 87 should replace the Fieseler altogether; the fewer varieties of aircraft carried reduced the number of differing aircraft spares needed on board ship and simplifying the role for those responsible for keeping the machines in the air.

To reduce the carrier aircraft's exposure to the elements out in the

82   War planes of the third Reich-William Green

83   It had always been possible to launch the Ju 87 by catapult in the role of bomber, but there had been problems in getting the torpedo fixture to withstand the strain of catapulting. This new fixture was still not considered capable of withstanding the shock of landing on the carrier's deck when carrying these weapons, any unused torpedoes having to be jettisoned prior to landing.

84   The aircraft was easily capable of landing without the use of the arrestor wire (though it did have a hook for braked landings as in normal operation the carriers decks would be cluttered with both men and machines).

85   Between them, these two aircraft were responsible for deploying most of the 40 tons of chlorosulphonic acid (a smoke generating liquid used to create smoke screens to hide the movements of the aircraft carrier from attacking enemy warships) carried on board the ship, some being reserved for use by the ship itself. Eight 600 kg containers were stored pre-filled with this liquid ready for use by the two designated aircraft. Slung outboard at the ship's stern for safe storage, from here the containers could easily be jettisoned overboard in the event of any damage without hindering carrier operations.

harsh Atlantic conditions, when not in an operational area *Graf Zeppelin's* aircraft would not routinely be kept on deck, but would have been stored in the hangars below. At all times the operational readiness of up to eight aircraft would have been maintained below decks by steam pre-heaters that would keep the aircraft engines, void of oil, heated to 70°C. The engine oil for these aircraft would only be added just prior to deployment, it too having been heated in its storage vessel at the front of the hangar, from where it was collected in drums that would be pushed over to the aircraft and decanted into the engine by a hand pump, thus avoiding cold starts of the aeroplane engines. This status could be maintained out on the flight deck by electric pre-heaters fed from power points on the deck, keeping the engines warmed up and ready to go.

Armament of aircraft ready for deployment whether with torpedoes or bombs would almost always take place below decks using the same equipment as a land-based airfield. Thus, aircraft would arrive on deck armed, fuelled and except for a motionless engine, ready to take off. The aeroplane's engine would have only been started once out on deck due to the lack of ventilation inside the hangars, but, being pre-heated and filled with oil already warmed to 60°C, this late start would cause no delay, the aircraft being ready to take off immediately upon the starting of its engine.

Once on deck, four-metre-high windshields, constructed of steel and perforated by many slits, provided windbreaks to break up and stop the wind, giving cover to man and machine for a distance of about 40 metres behind it. Two such shields were on deck, one at the bows for the aircraft on the catapult and one mid-way along the deck for those about to make a running take-off. When the aircraft were ready for deployment the shields could be quickly dropped to lie flat on the deck for the aircraft to pass over.

Unlike the British and American carriers, on which aircraft were secured to the deck by hooks and lashings, the *Graf Zeppelin's* aircraft would either be mounted on their catapult launching trolley, or, for the aircraft making a running take-off, as their position would only be temporary, held only by chocks.

Though not originally planned for the carrier, by 1942 it had been considered necessary to add a 'Fighter Defence Command'. Operating almost independently from the offensive 'Air Operations Room', Fighter Defence Command was responsible, as its name suggests, for the aircraft dedicated to the defence of the ship and would operate both fighter and smoke-laying aircraft to this end. The Commander (flying) would be based close to the Fighter Defence Command in the Air Operations Room, from where the long-range bombing operations of the fighters and torpedo bombers would have been controlled. Knowledge of weather conditions being essential for the successful and safe operation of aircraft, a meteorological room was also attached to the Air Operations Room.

Monitoring events in the air from his post in the Air Operations Room, the Commander (flying) would have been able to communicate via radio transmitter with airborne aircraft, his presence being felt all over the ship via telephone, communication with the aircraft handlers out on deck being transmitted over loud-speakers distributed along the flight deck. Being an essential command post on board the ship (indeed the ships whole existence was for the operation of this post and its aircraft), the Air Operations Room was organised like a chart-room and was equipped with a compass repeater, log (giving the ships speed), course plotter, airscrew revolution counter and meteorological instruments such as barometers, barographs and anemometers.

Understandably the Commander (Flying) held a very important position on board ship. He would be the equivalent of a gunnery officer on a battleship and be able to question the Captain's wisdom in the operation of aircraft; it would be he who would deal with flying offences, but for general problems with Air Force staff he would have to inform the First Officer (Navy).

As it was envisaged that the Captain of the ship would often be present in the Air Operations Room, there was direct communication with the engine room. For the tactical side of operations to help follow what was going on in the air, there was a plotting table, blackboard and a cupboard for storing maps and charts. A divan bed was available to the Commander allowing him to rest when on operations without leaving his post.

Control of the 'runway' would be the responsibility of the 'Flight-deck Control'. Situated with a commanding view of the flight deck, it was to have been inhabited by the Officer in Charge (O.C.) of Flight-deck Control and four operators. Flight-deck Control, like the Air Operations Room, was connected to the ship's telephone system and for other signalling purposes was equipped with signalling pistols and Morse lamps. Reporting to the O.C. was the Officer responsible for the catapults; he would have been stationed so as to be in visual communication with the pilots and the catapult operators.

An aircraft sitting on the launching track would be almost on top of the two compressed air cylinders that fed the whole catapult system. These giant cylinders required electric heating to maintain a temperature of about 20°C, as the venting of the enormous amount of gas needed to accelerate an aircraft up to 140 kmh over such a short distance would cause ice to form on the pipe work and essential control equipment. Laying between the two rails of the catapult in their own 'Alphol' insulated compartments just below the deck, the cylinders were almost 12 metres above the armoured deck that constituted the floor of the lower hangar, and were thus susceptible to the effects of falling shells or bombs detonating in or around these compartments. This was an exposed position considering the catastrophic effects that would have resulted were one to receive either a direct or indirect hit and explode.

Strapped into his aircraft mounted on the launching rails, one of the pilot's last acts prior to catapulting would be to grasp the control rod and pass his middle finger at the same time through the running knot of a strap that was secured to a sliding ring on a small steel cable that stretched transversely beneath the instrument board. 'In this way no involuntary pull on the control rod is possible; while the lateral control (ailerons) remain free because the ring slides freely on the cable.'[86] After a brief period of enormous acceleration

A Bf 109 being catapulted

the aircraft would be airborne, free of its launching trolley, which would be carried below decks on a special track and pushed by hand back to the hangar.

The carrier aircraft were to benefit from continuous High Frequency (HF) communications with the ship, the Luftwaffe having insisted that the ship be able to guarantee this service up to a range of 320 miles. An airborne aircraft would have been able to maintain contact with the carrier via HF and Very High Frequency (VHF) radio, the *Graf Zeppelin* having five transmitters dedicated to aircraft operations, consisting of one HF transmitter of 800 watts, two 100 watt units and a further two one hundred

---

86 Based on a description of a system seen to be in use by Stuka pilots. (National Archive document: ADMT 19137).

watt VHF sets. Presumably in fear of friendly fire coming from other ships of the Kriegsmarine, it was considered desirable to be able to contact other ships of the fleet and for the planes to carry an automatic transceiver that would allow the carrier's radar service to recognise the incoming aircraft as friendly. On board the ship, besides the transmitting room, the aircrews also benefited from a room dedicated to navigational aids. This navigation room contained radio receivers and direction finding (DF) sets that could be used to direct lost aircraft back to the safety of *Zeppelin's* armoured walls, though at the O.K.M.'s own admission these services were still under development in 1942 due essentially to lack of carrier experience, a process that would no doubt have taken quite some time to resolve.

Other air force requests included bilateral communication between aircraft, and in order to calm concerns over navigation and direction finding a capability to communicate with shore establishments to get navigational help (though this would probably use the same equipment needed for the HF contact between carrier and aircraft already mentioned). The air force also requested that the carrier aircraft have DF sets so they could be radio-guided onto targets by other aircraft or submarines, equipment that the navy no doubt intended fitting to the carrier's aeroplanes since the Luftwaffe were renowned for poor navigation over water; shore based aircraft often reporting positions at sea with errors of 40–60 miles, the acoustic buoy known as a Schwan (Swan) having already being developed to counter this.[87] As well as the aeroplane's fixed frame aerial that allowed for a radio-guided flight towards the carrier, a similar apparatus to allow a radio-guided flight towards a long-wave transmitter was requested.

Attempts were made to ensure ship-to-ship communication between the various ships that made up the carrier Task Force by duplicating *Zeppelin's* wireless transmitter (WT) rooms. The first of these, located close to the bridge was Room 'A', equipped with three 800 watt transmitters, three HF wave receivers and one allwave receiver, and the second of these, Room 'C', was a duplicate of Room 'A' but securely located below the armoured deck of the lower hangar. The various communication requirements that came with operating a carrier had resulted in approximately 50–60 aerials cluttering *Zeppelin's* sides and superstructure, aerials that would be essential for maintaining contact with a returning aircraft, establishing friend or foe, and by working in cooperation with the array of radar sets whose aerials constituted part of the cluttered exterior of the ship, would help to guard her well-being.

Of course *Zeppelin's* radar, no matter how many differing sets she carried, could never have matched those of her enemies, unless its development, stopped by Hitler, had been reinstated, and much work carried out to close the gulf that now existed between Germany's radar and those of the Allied forces. Great emphasis was put on the 'radar search receiver' or

---

87 The Schwan acoustic transmitter, a VHF beacon, was developed for dropping from aircraft to home vessels and other aircraft onto convoys.

Funkmessbeobachtungsgeräte (F.M.B.) that she was to carry, a device able to pick up a radar signal and accurately locate its source long before the probing enemy had made a location. Two of these sets mounted forward and aft of *Zeppelin's* solitary funnel would each provide 180° of cover, searching the whole horizon, an auxiliary listening set backing up the work of these two devices. The F.M.B. was added as part of the revised programme for electronic protection that was instigated when it was realised that the original system, requiring at least 13 different aerials was insufficient, at best only providing ten minutes' warning of incoming enemy aircraft, too small a time scale to get her own aircraft in the air and in a position to intercept the incoming attackers.

As well as the F.M.B. the once great Seetakt would now be carried. Mounted high above the ship, the Seetakt would be modified to calculate the height of an approaching aircraft, its eight-ton bulk supported on top of a reinforced mast, two other similar sets searching the lower horizon for low-flying aircraft. This revised plan for electronic protection retained the aft-mounted radar set that was attached to the underside of the flight deck. Serving no defensive purpose this set was for guiding aircraft making a blind landing. Another far more 'low tech' aid to returning aircraft (and aircraft taking off for that matter), was the oil burner mounted at the bows. The black smoke generated by this burner, acting as a telltale, would indicate the wind direction to those on the bridge of the ship, and thus the direction in which the ship must be sailed for aircraft recovery…straight into it, steaming flat out so as to increase the air speed over her deck.[88]

For the approaching aircraft, wind speed was indicated by four arrows on the deck made up of clusters of round lights that illuminate for night landings. Via these arrows, eight wind speeds could be indicated. A returning aircraft touching down on the flight deck would have aimed to land on the circle painted on her stern that indicated the spot that would most likely result in one of the arrestor wires being snagged, bringing the pilot and plane to an abrupt stop. Other flight deck markings included two longitudinal lines painted on the deck, carving it into three operational areas, those of landing, preparation and taking off. With correct management, this division of the flight deck should have allowed an aircraft to land every two minutes.

For an aircraft approaching at night, a row of red lights along the stern and a single row of seven lamps down the length of each side of the ship outlines the flight deck, further assistance being provided to an approaching pilot by green and white deck lights, green highlighting the landing area and white, the arrestor wires.

Upon its return to the carrier, deck hands would have freed the arrestor wire from the aircraft's tail hook, the aircraft immediately taxiing over to the mid-ship's elevator to be struck below decks. During night-time operations, when the elevators were in use, blue light would have been

---

88 Even today carriers sail into the wind during aircraft take-off and recovery to gain maximum benefit from the wind speed over the deck.

used in the hangars so as to avoid white light funnelling out of the cavern-
ous elevator shafts, potentially dazzling a landing pilot or worse, drawing
the unwanted attention of enemy reconnaissance aircraft and warships. To
facilitate the seamless change from white to blue light, an automatic switch
on the lighting circuit switched off the 200 watt overhead white lamps at
the same time turning on the blue 40 watt bulkhead mounted lights. This
no doubt produced a very gloomy atmosphere in the hangars, these blue
lights being mounted 20 metres apart.[89] Once in the hangar, and assum-
ing it was not intended to immediately re-deploy the aircraft, as a safety
precaution its fuel would be removed and returned to the two large storage
tanks below, which between them could hold 220 tons of this ethylised
petrol. De-fuelling, like the fuelling process, was facilitated at numerous positions around the hangar by pipes that ran to and from the storage tanks,
allowing the fuel to be safely pumped away, the explosive vapours being
sucked away by a pipe attached to the aircraft's filling point. As part of this
return-to-hangar process, the aircraft's engine would be emptied of oil, this
being done by operating the ship's oil distribution pumps in reverse, the oil
being returned to the four large conjoined storage tanks, where it would
be mixed with the ten tons of aircraft engine oil that was carried on board
ship. Immediately prior to the aircraft's next mission, heated oil drawn from
these storage vessels would again be added to its engine.

Once drained of fuel and oil, virtually any task could be completed on
the newly retrieved aircraft, there being plans to carry spare wings, engines,
undercarriages and even spare fuselages, all of which could be replaced
within the confines of the upper hangar, the aft portion of which, being
dedicated to aircraft maintenance, was equipped with cranes for this purpose. Towards the bow, in the lower hangar, a well-equipped engine repair
workshop allowed for the partial overhaul of engines by air force personnel
(though there was no plan to install engine test benches) and for those engines that were beyond repair or in need of an overhaul, 12 complete spares
were to be carried in a store on the upper hangar deck. Though there was
to be no dedicated machine shop specifically for the manufacture of aircraft
parts, the ships workshop would take care of any jobs requiring the use of
machine tools.

On the hangar decks many precautions were in place for preventing and
tackling fire. The aviation fuel being highly volatile (at least one Japanese carrier would owe its loss to the mis-handling of aviation fuel) was of grave concern. As a result the single entrance to each hangar was under supervision so
as to prevent any personnel carelessly entering with a lighted cigarette or any
other items that might cause a fire. Ventilation systems ensured that vapours
from any spilt aviation fuel could not collect inside the hangar decks, the air
being changed six times an hour, rising to 40–50 times an hour in the elevator shafts, a space that left unchecked would act as a sump, collecting these

89 There were actually bulkhead lights every 10 metres but they alternated between blue light and
    white light the latter being emergency white lights powered by 24 volts D.C. supplied from ac-
    cumulators: Italian documents 1942, (National Archive document: ADMT 19137).

volatile vapours. Precautions against sparks included bronze tools that would not spark when struck, hermetically sealed lights (even when unscrewing an illuminated 200 watt overhead bulb, any spark would happen in an enclosed space) and sockets that were of the gas-tight type, requiring the socket to be switched off in order to remove the plug.

In the event of a fire, the automatic sprinkler system would burst into life, triggered by the heat of the inferno. If he didn't already know, the specialist Warrant Officer stationed in the Fire Control Centre would be alerted to the location of a fire by warning lights on a control panel that indicated where the sprinkler had become active. It would be his job to direct the damage control teams to attack the fire with a variety of devices from portable fire extinguishers to remotely operated 'hangar drenching systems', whichever was most suited to the job in hand.

Another responsibility of the fire control Warrant Officer was the lowering of the three fireproof partitions running laterally across the roof of each hangar. Similar to a roller blind, these partitions could quickly be lowered, dividing the deck into as many as four sections so as to contain a fire. Any crew still in the area about to be isolated would be alerted to their impending entrapment by an alarm, evacuation being through rooms to the side equipped with showers intended to extinguish burning clothes and flesh. Ventilation to such a combusting area would of course be shut down so as not to fan the flames, and then the inert blanket gas 'ardexine'[90] dispensed into the enclosed space. Preventatively, the damage control teams could shut off the aviation fuel delivery pumps, allowing gravity to draw the fuel back down the delivery pipe into the bowels of the ship and safely away from the fire, though as an added safety measure these pumps would shut off automatically if the integrity of the aviation fuel delivery lines was compromised.[91]

To keep a ship such as *Graf Zeppelin* operational, besides the maintenance crews responsible for maintaining and repairing the carrier and its aircraft, the ship would need an effective damage control team, and not just for the hangar decks. Capable of sweeping her own path for mines, she was also protected by a vast array of electronic devices from echo-ranging sets and hydra-phones manned by specially trained operators listening for prowling submarines and distant propeller noise to radar operators searching for approaching surface ships and aircraft. In any engagement *Graf Zeppelin* would have been a prime target for attack; the Allies would hunt her down wherever she went, and the ability to quickly contain any damage would be a matter of life and death for her.

The Channel dash in February of 1942 had proven that even a close group of heavily protected battleships, complete with destroyer screen and

90 Distributed throughout the ship, in 20 different locations, from boiler room to hangar deck, 'ardexine' was stored as a liquid, but, on leaving its storage vessel, evaporated creating a heavier than air atmosphere making it ideal for fighting fires in such enclosed spaces.

91 Any such compromises were detectable by containing the fuel pipes within another outer pipe pressurised to 4 bar with an inert gas, any drop in this pressure signifying a breach in the outer pipe and activating the automatic shut-off.

fighter aircraft protection, were susceptible to a determined attack. On this occasion several of the six attacking Fairy Swordfish torpedo bombers of 825 squadron, aircraft that would have been one of the *Graf Zeppelin's* main Fleet Air Arm opponents succeeded in flying through the barrage of protecting fighter aircraft and Flak. On a suicidal mission reminiscent of 'The Charge of the Light Brigade' and every bit as heroic, some of the painfully slow biplanes even came close enough to the German Battle Group to release their torpedoes, though on this occasion no hits were scored, and all the aircraft were brought down.

The air cover planned for the ships making the Channel dash consisted largely of Bf 109s, a minimum of 16 fighters being over the convoy at any one time – more than representing the total complement of fighter aircraft deployable by the *Graf Zeppelin* and demonstrating the unpredictability of such engagements. Had the *Graf Zeppelin* sailing in such a task force been faced by a massed attack of Swordfish, perhaps consisting of more than one carrier group, which similarly passed the aircraft of the 'Fighter Defence Command', she would be relying on both her own gunners and those of her escorting battleship to bring them down. Had she ever been completed, attaining operational readiness, she would have worked in tandem with a battleship, probably one or more of the ships that made the Channel dash (in fact after authorising the renewed construction of the *Graf Zeppelin* in 1942, Hitler had expressed his desire to form a German carrier task force consisting of *Tirpitz*, *Scharnhorst*, a carrier, two heavy cruisers and 12 to 14 destroyers).

The Kriegsmarine Chiefs of Staff clearly understood the need for a battleship to operate with a carrier, even stating as much.[92] 1/Skl (Seekriegsleitung) the operations division of the German Naval Staff, commented, 'aircraft carriers stand permanently under the protection of battleships,' adding that, 'therefore, aircraft carriers would also require no sea artillery for their own protection,'[93] a fact realised too late for the *Graf Zeppelin* on which much space had been dedicated to the relatively useless 150 mm naval guns and their infrastructure. Though each gun was capable of firing six 101 lb shells per minute at targets 13 miles away, the lack of ability for these guns to operate as A.A. weapons put the *Graf Zeppelin* at a distinct disadvantage in comparison to the Royal Navy carriers such as *Ark Royal*, whose 16 4.5-inch guns were all dual purpose and capable of operating against both surface vessels and aircraft. Ironically it is also a fact that the *Graf Zeppelin's* 150 mm guns had played a part in the delay in her completion owing to the fire control system for them being delayed.

Any increased anti-aircraft (A.A.) capability offered to *Graf Zeppelin* by a battleship would have been very welcome by 1942, as the experience of war demonstrated the need for a greater number of anti-aircraft weapons onboard a ship.

92 Recognising the inability of the Allies to operate carrier aircraft in foul weather, the tempestuous waters of northern Norway were one of the last operating grounds of the Kriegsmarine surface fleet, the aerial supremacy of Great Britain being nullified somewhat. Conversely the carrier *Graf Zeppelin* would have needed to operate with a battleship for protection when operating in just such weather.

93 Taken from 1/Skl's September 1942 comments on 'Aircraft Carriers in the Fleet Formation'.

Unfortunately there was little scope to increase the number of these weapons on board the carrier though there were plans to exchange the existing single 20 mm gun mounts for quadruple fixtures of these same weapons. Badly positioned, the heavy A.A. weapons (105 mm) that *Zeppelin* possessed, 12 in all,[94] were all mounted on the starboard side of the ship in twin turrets; positioned both forward and aft of the superstructure they could not engage aircraft approaching from port without firing across the flight deck, and they were mounted so high on the ship that they would be unable to engage lower-flying aircraft.[95]

As well as increasing the barrage of A.A. fire, a battleship would offer welcome firepower in the event of conflict with enemy surface vessels that managed to close the range on the group. In such an engagement a carrier's flight deck, its sole means of delivering its main weapon, the aerial bomb or torpedo, was vulnerable to plunging shells and could easily be put out of action by just a couple of well-placed hits. It wasn't just incoming projectiles that could render the flight deck inoperable; bad weather was more than capable of bringing operations to a halt, an unescorted carrier in either of these situations being in a dire position. HMS *Glorious* demonstrated the vulnerability of an unescorted carrier with an inoperable flight deck when, caught for reasons that still remain unclear without any aircraft in the air, her flight deck was put out of action early on in the encounter by a shell from *Gneisenau*. Her fate sealed, she was lost along with her accompanying destroyers.

In the event of any such attacks being driven home successfully against the *Graf Zeppelin* it would be the damage control teams that saved the ship. War experience had shown that a torpedo impacting on a ship's fuel bunkers often resulted in burning fuel oil spreading through the ship's boiler room and lower decks, incinerating all in its way. The effects of such a fire on board *Graf Zeppelin* had been minimised greatly by the compartmentalisation of the ship such as the separating of the ship's boilers into four separate rooms. Where possible, the inert blanket gas ardexine, dispersed throughout the ship in 20 different locations, would be used to fight fires in the enclosed spaces below decks. For any blazes out in the constant breeze of the flight deck, foam would be needed, dispensed both from hydrants situated at intervals along the side of the flight deck, and from large trolley mounted extinguishers.

94 This figure assumes the third turret forward of the bridge was finally added. Originally built with five 105 mm turrets, plans were apparently made for a sixth as early as 1939, though it was definitely not in place as of Nov 1941 when the Italian commission visited her. Quoted as having 12 105 mm guns in a 'K' office report of August 1942 it must be assumed that the intention was for its addition during the phase of work started in 1942.

95 The 105 mm guns were to have been mounted in pairs both forward and aft of the superstructure. Capable of firing on either side of the ship, the targets for these guns were selected by one of the ship's four 'fire control' stations. Target selection was compiled with the aid of data from one of the four 'fire control' turrets mounted on the starboard side of the ship, data travelling between the two via one of two distribution panels (one being held in reserve). Once the target was selected by 'fire control' this information was relayed to any of the five installations. With this method of aiming the guns, four targets could have been fired at simultaneously. An officer stationed near the bridge would have had overall responsibility for directing the fire from these and the other lighter weapons (which had their own predetermined sectors) and as such would be in telephone communication with the fire control stations and the various machine gun units (37 mm & 20 mm).

A pair of 105 mm guns in action on board Tirpitz. Photograph courtesy of the Imperial War Museum, London. Ref. HU50881.

Covered in wood and operating aircraft, the flight deck was vulnerable to fire, the effects of which, once the blaze was under control, would need rectifying. Damage control teams, perhaps whilst the vessel was still under attack, would have to make running repairs with gas cutting torches cutting away that of the deck that had become a hindrance to aircraft operations, effecting repairs with wood shored up from below, re-instating the airstrip. It was planned to use asbestos matting, salvaged from a British cruiser, to plug any smaller holes, preventing any burning embers on the enclosed hangar deck below from being fanned back to life.

Besides structural damage, damage received to the unarmoured flight deck or the lightly armoured upper works of the ship from projectiles and falling ordinance could easily result in the loss of the onboard telephone network essential to aircraft operations. Lacking any armoured protection, the telephone wires would be very susceptible to flying shrapnel, and easily severed. In the event of such damage, 'field telephones' would come into play, rapidly connected to the network by 'field cable' stored on drums and easily reeled out; portable generators, batteries and reels of cable rectified similar problems with the power supply.

In the event of a devastating strike on the lightly armoured bridge or other communication failure, the Officer in Charge of the arrestor wire, having direct telephone communication with the engine room and the emergency rudder, could have maintained control of the ship, perhaps steering away from the action to run for safety, or altering course by steering into the wind to retrieve returning aeroplanes.

Built to the 'Tirpitz Principal', even without effective damage control, a ship as compartmentalised as the *Graf Zeppelin*, like all of the modern Kriegsmarine Capital ships, once secured for action with its bulkhead doors battened down, would have been a tough vessel to put on the seabed, as events in the future would demonstrate.

End of a Giant

SOVIET WAR BOOTY

Abandoned in the Mönne, it was not long before the advancing Russian armies over-took the derelict *Graf Zeppelin*.

It is easy to imagine the excitement of the conquering Soviet troops as they approached what would at first have appeared to be an intact aircraft carrier; perhaps only once she was boarded would the damage have become apparent. With inverted elevators, the first telltale sign that all was not well, it may well have been only when they went below decks and saw the water inside the hull that they realised that she was sat on the bottom of this shallow tributary.

No doubt eager to see if such a vessel could ever sail under the flag of the Red Banner Fleet, it would not have been long before Soviet engineers were looking to raise her. They would soon set about welding up the damaged bulkheads and various other perforations in the hull before pumping the entrapped water out.

Before the year was out (in fact by September of 1945) she would be floating once again in the shallows of Stettin, but as the Iron Curtain descended over Eastern Europe, the fate of Germany's sole carrier would become a mystery. Tales abounded about her. Some claimed that she was commissioned into the Soviet navy, others that she was loaded with sections of submarines and other war booty before being taken under tow to Russia, striking a mine en-route and sinking in the Gulf of Finland, the truth would not come out until long after the collapse of the Soviet empire. A letter from The Department of External Relations of the Ministry of Defence of the Russian Federation received by the author in September 2001 finally brought the matter to a close. It stated:

In answer to your letter of 21ˢᵗ May this year. I write to inform you that according to the documents of the archive the following information has been found:

The aircraft carrier Graf Zeppelin was damaged and scuttled by the German forces at the time of the retreat from Stettin, which is now part of the Polish Republic. It was raised by the Soviet Fleet between August and September 1945. In accordance with the decision of the Troistvenny Naval Commission on the disposal of the German Fleet. The aircraft carrier Graf Zeppelin, as a ship that was assigned to category "C" it underwent destruction on the 18ᵗʰ August 1947 at 18:08hrs. It was sunk in the Baltic Sea at Latitude **° **' Longitude **° **'

With Respects
The head of the Central Naval Archives
Captain of the 1st Rank I Shchetin

МИНИСТЕРСТВО ОБОРОНЫ
РОССИЙСКОЙ ФЕДЕРАЦИИ
★
ЦЕНТРАЛЬНЫЙ
ВОЕННО-МОРСКОЙ
А Р Х И В
„ 2 „ июля 2001 г.
№ 13402

18355, Ленинградская обл.,
г. Гатчина, Красноармейский пр., 2

Steve Burke

Уважаемый господин С.Бурке !

На Ваше письмо от 21 мая сего года сообщаю, что по документам архива установлено следующее:

Авианосец "Граф Цеппелин" был повреждён и затоплен немецкими войсками при отступлении в г. Щецин, ныне Польская республика. Советским Военно-Морским Флотом в августе-сентябре 1945 года он был поднят.

В соответствии с решением Тройственной военно-морской комиссии по разделу флота Германии, авианосец "Граф Цеппелин" как корабль, отнесённый к категории "С", подлежал уничтожению. 18 августа 1947 года в 18 ч. 08 мин он был затоплен в Балтийском море Ш = ♣   Д = ♠

С уважением !

Начальник Центрального военно-морского архива
капитан 1 ранга

И.Щетин

Letter received by the author from the Russian Ministry of Defence.

Elaborating on this brief description of the *Graf Zeppelin's* end, an article from a Russian web site, accompanied by a fantastic series of grainy photographs both apparently drawn from a magazine is summarised here. The article makes it apparent that back in April of 1945, sinking *Graf Zeppelin* was not the worst damage the retreating Germans had done to their carrier: all the major pieces of kit on board her had been destroyed; her elevators were almost inverted by the blast that destroyed them; her turbines and boilers had been destroyed, as had her power plants. Ignited in the confines of the below-decks area, the blast from each of these demolition charges had ripped and buckled the surrounding bulkheads, walls and ceilings as it radiated outwards from its epicentre, the flight deck was buckled and below-decks was in chaos.

In post-war Europe, vast amounts of surplus war materials lay scattered around the continent, and the victorious powers agreed at the Potsdam conference after the war how it would be disposed of. Having already raced to obtain for themselves those items such as the revolutionary type 21 submarines and Von Braun's missile technology on which research was to continue, the rest was categorised into those materials that would be kept, those that were to be divided between the victors and those which would be scrapped—as was the fate of many of the remnants of Germany's navy.

The Potsdam conference concluded that, 'The usable surface ships of the German fleet, including all ships which can be put into this condition within a specified time, together with 30 submarines shall be divided between the three allied powers in equal amount. The rest of the German fleet will be destroyed.'

Graf Zeppelin was now a decrepit ship of obsolete design, unsuited to modern aircraft, needing still months of work just to make her seaworthy. Under the agreements made at Potsdam, *Graf Zeppelin* would fall into Category 'C', that is sunken, damaged or unfinished ships which require more than six months of repair in a German shipyard to obtain completion. The Tri-commission consisting of Britain, America and Russia, declared that all warships of group 'C' should be sunk in a great depth of water or scrapped within a set period of time.

Graf Zeppelin was spared the wrecking ball and gas torches that would have cut and smashed her into pieces, erasing her existence and ensuring her anonymity forever by decree number 601 issued by the Soviet government. Appearing in 1947, this decree came from the government as notification 'for the destruction of the former German warships of category 'C' in 1947'.

The Soviet's chosen method for disposing of her was to use her as a weapons target, no doubt to gain knowledge about aircraft carriers, a type of vessel about which Russia knew nothing having never operated one, but which her soon-to-be enemies, the USA and Great Britain, possessed many having used them to great effect in the recent war.[96]

On 17 August 1947, the condemned vessel was towed out of Stettin for the last time and into the Baltic Sea, a sea from which she had never left. She

---

96 Following a similar tack to what Raeder had recommended to Hitler before the commencement of World War II, Russia would not try to compete with surface ship numbers, but would move towards the stealth of the submarine, a great many being built in the post-WWII era.

already had several shells and bombs embedded in her, which would be detonated remotely when she was over the designated zone for sinking – namely a section of water over 100 metres deep. Her lethal cargo consisted of a 1000 kg aerial bomb suspended inside her funnel and a further three 100 kg bombs and two 180 mm artillery shells placed at various points around her flight deck. Once these devices were detonated, expert military personnel who assessed the damage done and carried out the most rudimentary damage control boarded her. A second wave of experiments followed in which a further 1000 kg aerial bomb was detonated on her flight deck; she was again boarded for assessment before the third and final of these 'static tests' which consisted of the detonation of a 250 kg aerial bomb and two more 180 mm artillery shells, the same routine of boarding and inspecting again being followed.

The next phase of the weapons test consisted of an aerial assault that served only to demonstrate the inadequacy of the Soviet Air Force, and corroborate German wartime tales of the ineffectual nature of Russian aerial attacks against their ships. After an embarrassing series of attacks in which nearly 100 bombs were dropped, supposedly aimed at a 20 x 20 metre cross painted on her decks in five-metre wide stripes, only six would strike the ship and, of these, one failed to explode. Of the six confirmed hits only one of these bombs did any real damage, tearing a hole of about one-metre diameter in the deck; the other bombs being only 50 kg devices were much too small for this purpose and only succeeding in dinting the deck 5–10 cm. Though the pilots insisted that they had scored five more hits than they were credited with (11 in all), arguing that a number of their bombs landed in holes made by the static trials, this was still a poor tally for such a scale of attack against a huge, unarmed and static vessel, to which they did no damage that would have put her out of service for anything but the briefest of time.

Lacking any anti-aircraft fire and dead in the water, *Graf Zeppelin* had survived virtually unscathed a massed aerial attack, launched from the killing zone of 2070 metres (an area of intense anti-aircraft barrage in a real combat). Embarrassingly, three aircraft were lost as a result of this 'attack', forced to ditch in the sea. It is not known if one of the circling Catalina flying boats rescued any of these aircrews, there being two of these aircraft orbiting the scene: one as a Search and Rescue aircraft the other operating as a Command aircraft.

As this protracted weapons test continued, the weather started to deteriorate. The *Graf Zeppelin* had been hauled out of Stettin on a calm clear day, but conditions had already deteriorated by that very evening and as 18 August dawned the skies were heavily overcast and the wind had got up to 27 knots, blowing the carrier back across the Baltic towards Poland[97] and into shallower water. The Vice Admiral in charge of operations took it upon himself to bring the giant's suffering to an end. There would be no tests with mines as was planned, she would be sent to the bottom immediately. Calling in the torpedo boats (Type Elko) *TL-248, TL-425 and TK-503, TL-248* attacked first, but her torpedoes ran too deep passing under the keel. A second attack 15 minutes

---

97   A fact that is supported by weather maps of the Baltic over this time period.

later by *TK-503* scored a hit on the starboard side destroying the counterpoise bulge, though as designed, the armoured belt beneath it was left undamaged. The *coup de grâce* was delivered by one of three vessels that arrived an hour after *TL-248* had started the surface attacks. Of these three boats *Slawnij*, *Strogij* and *Strojni* (which it is believed were all submarines, though some sources describe as being destroyers) it was the *Slawnij* to which went the honour of sinking the aircraft carrier, the last of the twentieth century to be sunk by conventional weapons. The torpedo launched by *Slawnij*, like that fired by *TK-503*, struck the starboard side, but this time penetrated the hull. This was the blow that finally finished off the *Graf Zeppelin*. Slowly she started to list to starboard and her bows dipped. Within 15 minutes this list had increased to approximately 25° and after the passing of another eight minutes she was gone.

The Graf Zeppelin today. Here we see the companion way that ran along the starboard side of the ship. Courtesy of the Cmdr' Dr. Eng' Adam Olejnik , Department of Diving Technology and Underwater Work. The Military Naval Academy In Gdynia Poland

Lost and forgotten for some 59 years, *Graf Zeppelin's* location was hidden by the dark waters of the Baltic Sea and the Iron Curtain that had quickly enveloped it after the war. She would only be re-located in June 2006 when Poland, freed from the chains of Communism, as one of the world's newest capitalist states, was sourcing what capitalists need most…oil. Their research vessel stumbled across her remains, lying in a little over 80 metres of water, some distance away from the 113 metres that had been designated as her last resting place.

Image of a 20 mm gun mount on the wreck. Courtesy of the Cmdr' Dr. Eng' Adam Olejnik, Department of Diving Technology and Underwater Work. The Military Naval Academy In Gdynia Poland

Epilogue

To build a carrier

Serving to demonstrate both the inexperience and the genius of her designer, *Graf Zeppelin* was a showpiece of German engineering. Though she had some obvious faults,[98] she also exhibited many novel features, such as: modern control equipment in place of the traditional helm wheel, her helmsman altering course not with a wheel as had been the case for time immemorial, but by depressing a plunger that operated hydraulic control equipment, one plunger to turn to port and one to turn to starboard. Built by the Brown Boveri Company (who also built her turbines) and widely in use with Germany's U-boats, the more traditional helm wheel was now purely a backup device; two Voith Schneider bow thrusters were necessary to navigate the Kiel Canal but were also capable of providing forward motion of up to four knots in the event of the loss of her main engines.

These bow thrusters consisted of a rotor casing fitted with a number of axially parallel blades that rotate about a vertical axis, each of the propeller blades performing an oscillating motion about its own axis to generate thrust. When not in use, these whisk-like propellers retracted into a bell cavity in the bottom of the hull, a watertight door closing behind them. Controlled from the bridge, the sideways thrust from these multi-directional thrusters could have been

The Voith propeller as it would have looked in the lowered position. Thrust is generated by each of the whisk-like blades oscillating about its own axis. The direction of the thrust is given by rotating the blades about a vertical axis (the black ring). Courtesy of Voith Schneider

---

98 Such as excessively large casemate mounted 150 mm guns, whose lack of ability to operate as A.A. weapons put *Graf Zeppelin* at a distinct disadvantage to the Royal Navy carriers such as *Ark Royal*, whose 16 4.5 inch guns were all dual purpose, capable of operating against both surface vessels and aircraft.

used at speeds of up to 12 knots to overcome the effects of a jammed rudder such as that which proved the battleship *Bismarck's* undoing.

Other German developments for carrier operations included the compressed air catapult and the electric brake for arresting incoming aircraft over a very short distance. Not at all a novelty, the brake was essential for carrier operations. Based on the Japanese design that they were shown during the 'K' office excursion to that country, with typical German ingenuity the brake's design was improved so that Von Tirpitz himself would have approved of it, building into it a mechanical brake that would ensure that above all else the brake would keep working! Another idea for shipboard equipment borrowed from the Japanese, but proving far less favourable than the arrestor system, was the 'landing searchlights with three beams'. Extensively researched, the various developments of this concept were rejected as unsuitable for their intended use: Korting's attempt being too bulky and the colour separation insufficient. A later development by Zeiss Ikon using a catoptric system of separating the coloured beams whose order of appearance and angular width (in elevation) was:

The Zeiss Ikon 'landing search light with three beams'.

Green light beam	20°
White light beam	7°
Red light beam	18°

The three colours constituting the beam appeared with the lowest of the lights, red, being positioned so as to still be visible below an angle of 3° above the level of the flight deck. Two of these lights would have been placed at the aft end of the flight deck, so that their beams would converge at an angle of 40°. These beams, having a 40° horizontal spread resulted in the contemporaneous visibility of the two lamps extending along the beam, though not extending beyond the width of the flight deck. Interesting technology, but according to the test pilots at the Experimental Centre, absolutely inadequate.

Many companies who are still in existence today worked on the vessel, companies such as Demag who made the brakes and Siemens and A.E.G. who carried out studies to develop suitable flight deck lights, both attaining working examples, though A.E.G.'s lights were the clear favourite. The visibility of A.E.G.'s lights were declared 'generally satisfactory' having been viewed from a distance of 300 metres and a height of 15 metres (the approximate height of the flight deck above the water line); they were cleared for installation on the German carrier, and later offered to the Italians for use on their carrier, *Aquila*.

Detailed studies into every aspect of carrier operations were carried out, personnel numbers were known and specific roles for the crew identified, space being found for those men we don't usually think of as being on board a warship such as plumbers, carpenters, cobblers and varnishers. These studies both identified and corrected problems with the distribution of hot food (a problem on a vessel as large as the *Graf Zeppelin* with its maze of passages), it being arranged for distribution points around the ship where the food could be kept warm while awaiting collection, but even then it was calculated to take 40 minutes to get the food from the kitchens to these mess halls. For those problems of a more technical nature, full-scale mock ups were built, there being a replica of the carrier's boiler room, wooden replicas of her flight deck and amongst other things her hangar deck, complete with working elevator.

In order to study problems incurred during take-off and landing, to aid development and to help eliminate problems that might arise later with the real thing, a flight deck was built onto a ship of 'moderate tonnage', from which a light aircraft was flown, and of course there was the brake installed at the Travemünd airfield, where literally thousands of practice landings were made.

Numerous tests were carried out on models of the vessel to see the effect of eddies caused by everything from the superstructure to the flight deck, tests that resulted in the maintaining of the superstructure to as small an area as possible and the 'inner surface of the island…[being]…absolutely smooth in order to avoid eddies which would be very dangerous on the flying deck.' Even the flight deck curved down at the extreme stern of the vessel, to avoid creating turbulence for an approaching aircraft (and to reduce the risk of the aircraft's arrestor hook or tail wheel being damaged by impacting on the back of the ship).

Another test carried out using a model of the vessel involved heading the model at varying angles to the wind in order to establish 'the relative directions of the wind into which is not advisable to make landings'. A study of the smoke coming out of the funnel, already 13.5 meters high, demonstrated that it was liable to descend onto the stern area of the flight deck, hindering operations, highlighting the necessity to add a device for deflecting the smoke upwards as it departed the funnel.

The Kriegsmarine was always ready to tweak and adapt in response to experiences gained from wartime operations of those assets that the navy utilised and from information gained from other nations both Axis and Allied. As a result, over her life, *Zeppelin*'s crew levels fluctuated, the numbers of her guns and the amount of ammunition for those guns changed, even the numbers and type of aircraft desired for operations from the vessel changed. Throughout the *Graf Zeppelin's* war, only one thing remained constant: Herman Göring's lack of assistance with anything naval.

When the carrier was finally laid up in 1943 those aircraft that had been assembled for her[99] were not given over for naval use but on the whole were returned to Luftwaffe units or assigned for research and development work. Coming with their own tales, they constitute another book but in brief here is their fate[100]: three of the Fieseler's went on to be used as test aircraft the rest being sold to Rumania, after which nothing else is known of them; the 60 Bf 109Ts, built under contract by Fieseler, were stripped of their catapult points and arrester hooks and re-designated as T-2s. They served in Norway from where their elongated wings gave them the shorter take-off needed from the makeshift runways in operation there, runways that were of a similar scale to the carrier's deck. Transferred to operate from the island of Heligoland they fought on until the end of 1944, by which time all had disappeared from the Luftwaffe's books. Of all of the carrier aircraft that were built, it is the Stukas which have the most interesting of tales to tell, seeing action in the opening phases of the war, when planes of the newly formed carrier group 186 were called upon to attack Poland. Later, once construction of the carrier ceased some of the aircraft were used in experimental roles and some were returned to front-line units, but Erich Gimpel[101] planned the most intriguing use for these carrierless aircraft: Aided by the Stuka's folding wings the plan involved stowing two of these aircraft, dismantled in a submarine, transporting them to a Caribbean island for reassembly and flying them off on a mission to bomb the dam that held back the water for the Panama Canal. Potentially 'Operation Pelican', as it was called, could have put the canal out of action for years to come, the result being weeks added onto convoy routes for all shipping coming from the west coast of the USA. The mission was cancelled, just as the U-boats were ready to sail.

The Kriegsmarine's battle against the Luftwaffe for the control of the maritime skies was by no means unique to Germany; Britain's Royal Navy had experienced some similar difficulty when its naval air arm was transferred to the R.A.F. in 1918. The transfer created a rivalry that was to exist between the Admiralty and R.A.F. until the establishment of the navy's Fleet Air Arm (F.A.A.) in 1937, a 19-year period in which the Royal Air Force's obsession with strategic bombing resulted in little development of maritime aircraft, leaving the Fleet Air Arm in the initial phases of World War II operating inferior aircraft to those of other countries. Germany's lack of ability to

---

99   Under direct orders from Hitler himself as a result of the 1942 plan to expand the carrier fleet.

100 It has not been my intention to go into any great detail in this book about the aircraft intended for carrier operations, though for readers who are interested, William Green's book: *Warplanes of the Third Reich*, would be a good starting place.

101 The man later famously caught in America operating as a spy in an attempt to steal America's atomic secrets.

sort this issue was greatly detrimental to their war effort, though in fairness to Admiral Raeder, Göring's 'colossal vanity' was a stumbling block that few could have passed. Obstructive in their actions, Göring's air force disposed of one-third of the aerial mines available to the navy by dropping them on British cities as demolition charges; halted construction of the F5 aerial torpedo without even discussing the issue with the navy; even depleted what few aircraft were available to the navy at every opportunity. Worse than this interference with maritime assets was the lack of co-operation exhibited by the Luftwaffe, carrying out operations on its own: attacking Allied convoys, with the aerial torpedoes that they now claimed the exclusive use of, scattering a convoy for the sinking of one or two ships, dashing the chances of U-boats that had spent perhaps days getting into a position to attack.

There were no doubt many in the Allied navies, both fighting and merchant who owed their lives to Göring and his failure to supply decent reconnaissance and carrier aircraft. Equally many a man in the Kriegsmarine would owe his life to the fact that the carrier was not completed in compliance with Hitler's March 1942 order, for by then *Graf Zeppelin's* chance of glory had passed. At one time capable of altering the course and maybe even the outcome of the war, by 1943 (the earliest she could have been completed) both the vessel and her aircraft were outdated and outclassed, the Allies had complete aerial superiority over the Atlantic; she would have been hunted relentlessly until she, like so many other vessels, rested on the seabed along with much of her crew.

For the *Graf Zeppelin* as with all showpieces, others would look with envy to see what innovations they could borrow for their own uses; for the Russians the derelict carrier still exhibited many. No doubt scrutinised in the two years between her raising and subsequent disposal, a Soviet ship visiting British waters would indicate one of the technologies that was borrowed from the carrier; in 1955 the Soviet cruiser *Sverdlov* visited Portsmouth on a goodwill visit, of interest to both the British and US governments due to its incredible manoeuverability, it was secretly inspected whilst in Portsmouth harbour by non other than 'Buster' Crabb, the famous British wartime diver. As Crabb approached the bow he came across a large bell-like cavity; upon entering it he found housed within it…a retracting propeller, used as a bow thruster to push the bow sideways through the water facilitating sharper turns. As to what else they borrowed, only time will tell.

Bibliography

Aakra, Kjetil. & Kjaeraas, Arild. *CAMOUFLAGE & MARKINGS OF THE MESSERSCHMITT BF 109T IN NORWAY 1941 - 1944*, Print Konsult

Ballard, Robert D. *THE DISCOVERY OF BISMARCK*, Madison Press Books, 1990

Ballard, Robert D. *RETURN TO MIDWAY*, Madison Press Books, 1999

BEKKER, C.D. DEFEAT AT SEA, Ballantine books, 1955

Breyer, Siegfried. *THE AIRCRAFT CARRIER GRAF ZEPPELIN*, Schiffer Military History, 1989

Cajus, Bekker. *THE GERMAN NAVY 1939–1945*, Chancellor Press, 1974

Crawford, Steve. *BATTLESHIPS AND CARRIERS*, Dempsey-Parr, 1999

Dönitz, Karl. *MEMOIRS*, Da Capo Press, 1997

Green, William. *WARPLANES of the THIRD REICH*, Purnell Book Services Ltd, 1970

Grove (Editor-in-Chief), Eric. *GREAT BATTLES OF THE ROYAL NAVY*, Bramley Books Ltd, 1994

Hädeler, Wilhelm. FLUGZEUGSCHIFFE, J.F. Lehmanns Berlag, 1939.

Haines, Gregory. *DESTROYERS AT WAR*, Book Club Association

Harrison, W.A. *FAIRY SWORDFISH AND ALBACORE*, The Crowood Press Ltd, 2002

Humble, Richard. *AIRCRAFT CARRIERS THE ILLUSTRATED HISTORY*, Winchmore Publishing Services Ltd, 1982

Isby (editor), David. *THE LUFTWAFFE AND THE WAR AT SEA 1939–1945*, Chatham Publishing, 2005

Jackson, Robert. *HISTORY of the ROYAL NAVY*, Parragon, 1999

MacDonald, Scott. *NAVAL AVIATION NEWS (1962–1963)*

Marshall, Francis L. *SEA EAGLES, Air Research Publications*, 1993

Middlebrook, Martin. & Mahoney, Patrick. *BATTLESHIP*, Penguin Books, 1977

Porten, Edward P. Von der. *GERMAN NAVY IN WORLD WAR TWO*, Pan Books, 1972

Raeder, Erich. *GRAND ADMIRAL*, Da Capo Press, 2001

Ruge, Friedrich. *DER SEEKRIEG THE GERMAN NAVY'S STORY 1939–1945*, U.S. Naval Institute, 1957

Ruge, Friedrich. *THE SOVIETS AS NAVAL OPPONENTS*, Patrick Stephens Ltd, 1979

(Forward by) Showell, Jak P. Mallman, *FUEHRER CONFERENCES ON NAVAL AFFAIRS 1939-1945*. Greenhill Books, 1980.

Showell, Jak P. Mallmann. *GERMAN NAVY HANDBOOK*, Sutton Publishing Ltd, 1999.

Showell, Jak P. Mallmann. *GERMAN NAVY IN WORLD WAR TWO*, Naval Institute Press

Smith, Peter C. *THE SEA EAGLES*. Greenhill Books, 2001

Treadwell, Terry C. *STRIKE FROM BENEATH THE SEA*, Tempus Publishing, 1999

Trevor-Roper (editor), H.R. *HITLER'S WAR DIRECTIVES 1939–1945*, Sidgwick and Jackson, 1964

Tute, Warren. *THE TRUE GLORY*. Bloomsbury Books, London, 1983.

Westwood, J.N. *FIGHTING SHIPS OF WORLD WAR II*, Book Club Association

Wood, Tony. & Gunston, Bill. *HITLER'S LUFTWAFFE*, Salamander Books Ltd, 1997

OTHER REFERENCE MATERIAL

Documents from the personal collection of Großadmiral Raeder (PG31320 & PG 31763) courtesy of the Naval Historical Branch (London)

Evaluation report No.76. 8 June 1945 (from the Imperial War Museum collection, Duxford)

BRITISH INTELLIGENCE OBJECTIVES SUB-COMMITTEE (BIOS) - FINAL REPORT No.s 28, 382, 509 & 1333 (Imperial War Museum collection, Duxford)

COMBINED INTELLIGENCE OBJECTIVES SUB-COMMITTEE – ITEM No 29 (FILE No. XXXIII-68) (Imperial War Museum collection, Duxford)

National Archive document: ADMT 19137 (referred to throughout this book as 'The Italian Document')

SHIPPIING WONDERS OF THE WORLD, (The Amalgamated Press Ltd)

And last but not least www.royalnavyresearcharchive.org.uk.

ISBN 142512216-7